# EMOTIONAL

# DETOX

If it was not for one of the darkest periods of his life, Dave Fraijo would have not been able to write this book that can pull those with emotional issues back into the light. Dave shares important details of his experience and provides practical guidance and keys for living a more powerful and peaceful life. This is a meaningful book with wise insight.

Rev. Lonnie Whittington
Staff minister, Creative Living Fellowship, Phoenix
www.creativelivingfellowship.com

David's voice brings to mind the words of the great Sufi teacher, Hazrat Inayat Khan who said, "The voice is not only indicative of a man's character, but it is the expression of his spirit." David not only shares his personal journey of evolution during which he recovered his spirit, but he offers insight and support so others may do the same. This is a book of hope and promise for anyone struggling with their inner demons.

Rev. Dr. Michele Whittington
Senior Minister, Creative Living Fellowship, Phoenix

By way of his remarkable story of recovery, resiliency and per- severance, David Fraijo provokes us to question what we believe to be true about ourselves and our place in the world, in the universe. He reminds us that we can remake and redefine ourselves as we release what was done to us.

You can experience yourself and your life with less judgment and more self-love.

Randy Webb, MA, MC, LPC, LMHC
Learning consultant, therapist, translator

A greatness that David Fraijo demonstrates in his writing, as well as in his everyday life, is his ability to connect with others by being just who he truly is. In his book, a combination of memoir and life guide, David invites us to accompany him on his path of awareness, struggle, and, at last, healing. Along the way, we can't help but recognize parts of ourselves. Through this immersion into David's redefinition of life, we come to understand the full meaning of his favorite quote, from Richard Bach's Illusions. "The bond that links your true family is not one of blood, but of respect and joy in each other's life." Welcome to the family.

Kathie Kelling
Evocator, inspirational facilitator

# EMOTIONAL

# DETOX

### Redefining Self

Moving past trauma to a new identity

# DAVID FRAIJO

Printed in the United States of America
Published by IRW Publishing

ISBN: 0692446796
ISBN-13 978-0-692-44679-9

Cover photo by Susan Nelson
Cover design by Patricia Grady Cox, IRW Publishing

I dedicate this book to all adult children of trauma and to anyone who has experienced an event that affected them in a powerful way. I dedicate this book to those who choose to question the identity they created in order to survive and are now beginning to question whether this identity is their SELF or something created from a collective perception of others, or from a family system that demands certain roles be played out in order to maintain perfect dysfunction.

I dedicate this book to those who are beginning to understand that their emotional discomfort is a part of the healing process and not an inherent defect or flaw.

David Fraijo

# THE CONCEPT OF EMOTIONAL DETOX

This book is my story. It's a story of my life, my addiction, my decision to heal myself. When we have an emotional attachment to behaviors that once supported us, we can let go by realizing there are physics and science behind that on a cellular level. We are biochemical electrical systems—in a way, a very sophisticated computer—but we have feelings and emotions and we make judgments about ourselves.

What is Emotional Detox? Am I rationalizing my disease/illness or is Emotional Detox a true concept? We sometimes choose to not pursue healing because we think the pain will be unbearable. For example, even though drinking had become hurtful to me and those around me, I believed that stopping would be more painful. It can be frightening to lose the only identity we've ever had, whether it's being a gang member or a veteran. All our self-identification may come from that association, but it may not be who we really are. There are other possibilities. There are choices.

> **Emotional Detox** begins when we recognize what our emotions are. Where did they come from? If our lives are not working, it's possible that our self-definition is the result of trauma. We create an identity that serves as a survival technique in order to deal with the traumas we've suffered.

I have come to accept the science behind the creation of disease, addiction, and depression and accept the science of healing. I have learned I can redefine my identity and move beyond toxic thoughts and energy to healing.

I'm writing this book for people like myself, who didn't get that.

If I had written this book before I went into treatment, its title would have been "My Name is David and I'm Bad." I had no idea I was alive. I was stuck in an emotional experience, full of moral judgment of myself. It felt bad.

I was in treatment many years ago. I stopped drinking many years ago. Yet I recently learned something about myself, when my daredevil partner Susan talked me into going on a hot-air balloon ride in Sedona. She had to talk me into it because of my fear of heights. I agreed to do it and found that I enjoyed it!

My lack of fear surprised me, and I mentioned this to the balloon pilot. When he dropped us off, he said a lot of people *think* they are afraid of heights. He can't even climb up a ladder and get on a roof, but he's not afraid of heights. It's actually *the edge* that people are afraid of.

That comment really affected me and I had to think about it for a couple of days. I realized that for years and years and years I always felt like I was on an edge. I tried all kinds of different things to get myself over that edge, onto the other side. I'd been sitting on an edge for decades in my recovery.

I don't feel like I'm on the edge anymore.

I hope you will choose to leave the edge. We are all power but sometimes we lose or give away our power. I gave my power away until I realized I am not powerless.

When I speak to groups, I'm sometimes asked if I'm a healer. I eventually came to recognize that people ask that because they are looking for someone to heal them. I don't want to take on that responsibility. You have to find your own path. I am a healer but I am my primary client. I would like everyone to recognize they are healers, with themselves as their primary client.

Maybe something in this book will resonate with you. If so, walk with me on the path, away from the edge.

You are a healer.

You can choose to heal yourself.

# THE PAST

## Childhood

I have three siblings and we are each five years apart in age. My oldest brother, at the time of my birth, was about 15. My mother was 36. My oldest brother was already acting out, which was his way of coping, as were my other brother and my sister. Add to this the toxic relationship my mother had with my father and her likely acute depression as well as a host of other diagnoses, and my mother was the perfect storm. She eventually shut down, setting up my second brother to be the caretaker of everybody. My sense has always been that I was just one more stressor to her ability to survive.

There are many powerful dynamics involving the different players in my family of origin. I am not going to attempt to define these for my family. Respectfully, I know they might have a different perception on specifics. I do know that when we have had the chance to be together, there seems to be a shared consciousness between us that it was pretty crazy for all involved. After our mother's transition to Source, I made a comment that coming from this environment, it was amazing that we turned out half-ass normal.

I have shared for many years the events that occurred on my life journey. Some were from my time with my family of origin. I have had few to no memories of some of these events. Others I could at least describe (some of them), but with little emotional connection to the event. One example of this is related to a time as a child, perhaps between the ages of ten to eleven.

My father had come home very drunk and very enraged. This was only one of the many times when my parents fought, which seemed to be often and always lasted for extended periods of time. It was not uncommon for their arguments to last for months. There were periods of what felt like deafening silence between my parents. Then as the tension grew, it would end with explosive verbal and physical violence.

Many such episodes followed the theme of my father wanting someone to inflict pain and injury on him. Understand that these patterns were developed from his own issues of childhood trauma, yet I did not know that at that young age, nor could I reason through it enough to resolve the toxic energy that I was absorbing in every cell of my body.

As I stated, there were many of these events. The one I am going to share with you now resulted in an extraordinary healing over 45 years later. From what I remember of that particular incident, when my father came home, I got a sense of what the night might be like by the sound of his truck door slam. As the tension grew and the arguing got louder, at some point in his blind rage he brought out a gun.

Again, following the pattern, he wanted my mother to shoot him. My role in most of these events was to do my best to somehow try to stop them, to somehow get in the middle, somehow get between them. But they only stopped when they were done. My continuous failed attempts created a long-time belief and perception of, "No matter what I do, it is never enough."

At some point in this melee, I got my hands on the gun. I have no recollection of whether I grabbed it, or it was set down. All I remember is running out of the house, gun in hand, down the street to Osborn Road. At some point I opened the gun to check the cylinder. The only emotion I recall from that moment, other than complete amazement, was incredible anger. The gun was not loaded. It was just a big show. I then realized that I was running down the street in cut-off shorts and tee shirt, barefooted, with a gun in my hand. So I put the gun in the waistband of my shorts and pulled my shirt over to hide it. At some point in this confused state of being I realized I needed to get to a place where I could think. I walked to my brother's home. I don't recall what happened after that. But I never forgot that incident.

## Dad

Much of what I know about my father is from stories I heard from him and others, and by observing how he interacted with others outside the family. There seemed to be quite a difference in those interactions. I struggle to have much recall related to him. I remember having a great deal of pride that he was in the pool deck business, and my pride was based on his being recognized as one of the best in town. Another source of pride is that he had a lot of history in Arizona. Of course, the main impact on me was how I perceived him at home, and for some reason, I do not have much recall of that, just a feeling that he was absent.

My mom told me that Dad was physically abused by his father, my grandfather. She told me that he had been kicked down stairs and beatings were regular.

My dad told a story of a man who was selling items out of a wagon. This man offered a cat o' nine tails (a small leather whip with nine straps at the end of it) to my grandfather. Dad said the man looked over toward him and then to my grandfather, and he felt they were somehow acknowledging that this would be what was needed to deal with my dad.

My grandfather purchased it and used it on my dad. Eventually, in order to survive, my dad became a runaway. I perceived, from the stories told to me, that my grandfather experienced a major shift within him when he came to this country from Mexico during one of the political conflicts, that somehow there was some shame in not staying to fight. This elevated or expanded his drinking.

I have studied addiction and I have often questioned whether this was a reason or an unconscious excuse. I know little to nothing about my grandfather's history. Based only on the behaviors that he exhibited, there had to be lots of trauma in his history. I recall several years into my own healing my father asking, "I wonder why he treated me like this." My response was, "I do not know, I just wonder what happened to him."

That caused my dad, perhaps just for that moment, to also wonder. Many of my dad's stories come from moving to Jerome, a mining town that was booming at the time. He was a lover of baseball and was, by all accounts, a very skilled player. He told stories of incredible batting averages and spectacular plays on the field. The feeling that came from him when he shared about this time was one of being honored by his teammates and those who watched him play. Many times he would meet old friends who had watched him play. My father would say how they commented on his extraordinary abilities on the baseball field. He seemed to be starved for this honoring of his past success. He talked of working delivering milk and also earning extra money by selling foods that were prepared by my grandmother. He knew where the Chinese immigrants had their opium dens. He sounded like he loved the entire Jerome adventure.

He told a story about one of his best friends being very sick, with little chance to survive. The boy's father hand-built a coffin for his son. But the friend lived. He, my dad and others ended up installing wheels and steering and making a soapbox car out what was supposed to have been his friend's coffin.

While celebrating my thirteenth birthday at a restaurant, my father told the story of his thirteenth year, much of which was spent suffering from pneumonia in the Jerome hospital. The story brought me to tears due to his childhood misfortune with ill health. It was not much of a celebration for me. He had a large scar on his back where the hospital did surgery to drain his lungs of infection. I later found a magazine with an aerial view of Jerome, by then a ghost town. At the center of the photo was the hospital. My dad showed me the window of the room where he stayed. I framed the picture and had it in my office for years.

I once took the family to Clarkdale for a ride on the Verde Valley train. On the drive from Sedona to the train station in Clarkdale, I noticed the town of Jerome high on a hill. I suddenly realized the distance between Jerome and Clarkdale, which made even more impressive my dad's accounts of walking down the hill on Friday afternoons from Jerome to Clarkdale to dance, drink and, by his accounts, fight, and then walk back.

Later in his life my father wanted to write his stories in a book. He recorded his recollections by reading what he had written, and hoped someone would help him with this process. I wanted to be that person, wanted badly for him to ask me to help him, but he never did. But I took what he had recorded and listened to his voice struggling through as he read. My sadness over how he glorified his and his friends' drunken brawls with one another was deep. It was a profound realization when I understood that these were his glory days. I brought back the recordings. He had not asked me to help him and, although I did not feel grateful for that at the time, I do now.

I feel my dad had great pride in the fact that his father was very advanced in the world of mathematics. My grandfather was a machinist in the mines and worked on the trains. He made tools and parts. The computer of the day was a slide rule. It was obvious my grandfather took great pride in his tools. At some point some of these tools were missing. A half-sister pointed the finger at my father who was severely beaten for this disrespect of these things that belonged to my grandfather. Years later, after the death of my grandfather, it was discovered that the tools had been hidden. My dad had not hidden them yet he had taken the severe beating.

My grandfather worked on some of the steam engine locomotives in Jerome. When mining slowed in Jerome due to the economy, one of those engines was sent to Superior, another mining town at the time. My grandfather also moved to Superior where, shortly after, he died of alcoholism.

My father's account of witnessing his father's death seemed to express a sense of freedom. He would not be beaten any more. I understand the conflicted feelings of wanting to honor my own father and letting go of the pain between us. My father, despite the memories of beatings, spoke with pride of how the engine his dad worked on was used at the end of a movie called How the West was Won.

That engine is now a permanent fixture at the McCormick Ranch Park in Scottsdale. A large part of my family went to the park to have our picture taken around the steam engine. We had also felt a sense of pride in our grandfather. We tried to understand his behaviors, and how they had affected my dad who carried the consequences of those behaviors with him the rest of his life.

My father was often open to do some things that would take him back to the glory years. He would go to the preseason baseball games as much as possible. On occasion, he would take me. His baseball history included being on the 1930 state championship team, and there is a picture of the entire team and coaches that he donated to the Jerome Museum. During a visit there, I stood with others who were viewing the photo and wanted to proudly tell them, "Look, that's my dad." But I was also filled with feelings of sadness over all the unresolved issues I had with him at that time. I will come back to this later as something powerful happened shortly after that period of time.

As a child I did not recognize Dad's influence over me, nor could I understand it to the degree I do now. It has taken decades of study and my desire to let the past go and heal. My dad's life was very adventurous and full of travel before and after the death of his father. It was the Great Depression and, with his father's death, it was up to him and his other brothers to support their mother. That trickled down to his relationship with who would later be his wife and my mother. They traveled a lot. Then I was the last to be brought into the family, and sometime after my birth he started his own company.

He was a self-taught man even though he did not finish grade school. He was very intelligent and had a tremendous curiosity about the world. He had a love of his connection to the Earth and mining. He loved his collection of mineral specimens.

While working in the mine in Superior, he helped start the union. He seemed to have the ability to bring people together in thought. From there he moved around and then settled in Phoenix. He told us that he created a set of plans to build a home. He would later joke about giving the plans away to others, missing out on being a land developer, missing out on other opportunities. Most of us have similar experiences. I know I have had my fair share.

I now understand that my missed opportunities were mostly due to fear; I can only speculate what it was for my dad. We had in common that we each started companies with little to no knowledge of how to run one. My dad could out-work any three guys, yet lacked the finesse of attending to the details. He was extremely nervous about certain aspects of the work he did. I also carry these genes. His nervousness would transform to aggression quickly. He was prone to enraged reactions. This is what actually motivated him to go and work on his own.

The story I heard is that while working for another company, he got into an argument with the owner or a supervisor. It escalated, and dad went after that person with a shovel. Fortunately, my older brother was working alongside our dad and stopped him. Soon after, my dad started working for himself, and my uncle went to work for him. My dad arranged the work and my uncle and brother, and other friends and family, would do the work. My perception is that my dad's time out in the field got smaller, and he spent more time in the bar.

Dad was well respected within the pool industry. He had a "good old boy" demeanor that played out well. But his playing the role of peasant/peon and his blind rage were qualities that pushed customers away. At a meeting for a minor complaint related to some work by his company, he went full blown. One homeowner said he was concerned that my dad was going to have a stroke in his backyard. I was deeply repulsed by my father's behavior, but it altered me in a way that benefited me.

I did my best to represent myself in my own business as articulate, intelligent, and without class envy. My dad played his own version of the race card in a self-demeaning manner. I do not feel that this gives any benefit to representing ourselves in our humanity or the culture we originate from. Even though I rejected this extreme, I carried my own version of this most of my life.

I remember my dad coming from work, after a stop at the bar, carrying a six-pack of beer. My recollections of that time are vague; it is not like I have any recollection of feeling excited to see him.

He could be volatile, but as time went on in his relationship with my mother, the fights seemed to slow down somewhat, at least according to my older brothers and sister. I cannot even imagine what it was like for them, if what I witnessed was "slowed down." This may have referred to my dad striking our mother. I had never seen this so I assume that at the later stages of their relationship, where I was a witness to it, some role reversal had taken place.

I witnessed Dad hitting himself in the face with closed fist and pulling out his hair. He called himself vulgar names, and stated it as though he knew this was what we felt about him. He requested my mother strike him, and she would sometimes follow through. Even more strangely, he used to try to straighten out the covers on the couches or fix the rugs.

Dad also attempted to get into fist fights with his sons. I was incapable of striking him, even though I held much disgust for him at that moment. I believe with all my heart that if I had played into this event with him, he would have used this against me later down the line. I ran away from home but only stayed away for a few days. It seemed that it was impossible to leave. My role was to always be in the middle, trying to stop their fights; I always wanted to somehow fix or help. Case in point: one time Dad got sick in the car, and even though the smell was making me ill, I tried to clean up the car.

Mom's behaviors were quite the opposite. There was a time when it was just the three of us, Dad, Mom, and me. Dad and I had contracted whooping cough and were beginning to recover, yet still had bouts of uncontrolled coughing. During one of these attacks,

Dad got dizzy and passed out near the bathroom door. As he fell, he hit his head on the edge of the door, cutting himself pretty badly. I heard him fall and made my way to him. He was bleeding and it looked to me to be bad so I called out for help. My mom was a short distance away. She never even looked up. For a long time I was angry with her, thinking he could have just died there on the floor, but he healed and we went on with our lives.

Many years later as I reflected on their relationship, I guess she had had enough and just did not care anymore. His behavior could get downright crazy. In one of their battles he went into their closet and ripped to shreds all of his clothes and threw them into the bedroom. I remember walking around the clothes that lay on the floor for days, wondering how to make some kind of sense out of it. I shared the lesson many years later with someone else: "You just can't rationalize insanity."

I constantly desired to be close to him. I wanted to be of some help to him, but instead we completed a cycle of frustration between us. He would say or do something that upset me, then I would do the same to him. I started to avoid doing anything with him. I was not able to give him any advice on how to make his work more effective and easier; he kept repeating the same way, doing it his way. My anger would become so huge that I would have to walk off.

There was this one time when he was loading a trailer, the kind that sets in the bed of a pickup. He insisted on backing up the pickup truck to the trailer in one way and it was not working. I tried to explain that just a slight turn of the steering wheel would make it work. By the time the truck was lined up correctly, his anger was so great—as was mine—that I left. He then attempted to finish loading it alone, and could have by lifting the trailer a little on both sides, one at a time; it would have been easy. Yet he cranked the trailer up totally on one side to the point that the trailer fell over on the side where he was working.

The only thing that kept him from being crushed was a block wall that stopped it from falling on him. Of course, I felt horrible for leaving but then I began to wonder if he had done this with some intent. It was not the only time he was willing to hurt himself in order to be a victim. Once with a gun and another with a knife, my mother played it out with him so she would look like the perpetrator, when it was really being set up by him. I believe this with all my heart as I had a role in one of these incidents.

I'm sure I could go on with other examples of how I perceived my dad, but it is not a desire on my part to beat up a dead man. I can't wish that anything could have been different, because this is the way it was.

Again, understand that these are my perspectives of this part of my life with my father. Were there good times? I'm sure there were, yet those did not mold me as much. My dad's life represented the life that he lived from his past. I really understand this in major detail.

There is one last experience that I would like to share. I had spoken earlier in this writing about Jerome and my dad's life there. We had taken a trip, my then wife and I, to Sedona. Part of that trip was to take the train ride into the Verde Valley. The train left from a depot in Clarkdale, which was just southwest of Jerome. After the train ride we decided to go to Jerome, so we did in the next couple of days.

The first stop was to the museum and there we saw the picture of my father and the baseball team he was a part of. A strong uneasiness came over me. I began to feel anger. I shared with my wife that maybe it was looking at how the owner of the mine lived. It was his opulent house that became the museum, and I had thoughts of my grandfather and the thousands who made him rich and the contrasting way they lived and how so many died. Then I wondered if I was picking up on those emotions from all those who lived there in the past. I also began to think about how I could be channeling my own father's angry emotions that he carried with him his whole life. So we left without any clear knowing.

We got home and within a few days my father died, alone in the bathroom with his face on the lid of the toilet. I never asked, but I wondered if my mother had heard anything and didn't go to help, if she had just had enough. I know in every cell of my body that my dad was part of an intergenerational system; I became a part of it; my adult children are a part of it. I am amazed and grateful that I have expanded in my healing from all this.

## Mom

These again are my own perspectives and may be totally different from someone else's perspective.

My mom was the youngest in her family. Her mother died before she could have any recollection of her. She had three older sisters and an older brother. They were very protective. One sister claimed that she would fight anyone who looked like a threat.

Mom, like my dad, grew up in extreme poverty. Her father, my grandfather, after the death of his wife, sent the girls to live with a cousin or uncle on what I guess was a little farm in south Phoenix. I remember stories that if anyone unknown to them came by our home, all the girls would hide in the trees. Mom would hide behind the blinds in the house.

She married my dad and it seemed their relationship was always strained, to put it lightly. She had five children of which one—a boy—died early in his young life. The four of us who remained are approximately five years apart, which I always thought made for some interesting dynamics for me while still inside her.

My mom traveled around with Dad and the kids as he worked in different places, but by the time I showed up they had settled in Phoenix. I lived in two homes before I moved out at nineteen years old.

My mom had a love for pets. She always had birds, fish, and dogs. In South Phoenix they had chickens and even geese. After they settled into the home that I spent most of my childhood in, she had collected a large number of birds, mostly canaries, but also myna birds and other exotics. There was never a lack of sounds coming from these birds.

She loved planting, and this was one of the positive times that we had together, as I would help dig and plant for her. Dad built a fish pond in the back yard, and she would spend hours cleaning and caring for the fish, as well as with the planting. I now understand that this was her time away from my father; this took her to a place where she could be out of the trauma. Yet there were many times, lost in her creations, that she would look up and there he was—watching her. This would really upset her, as would his constantly asking her where she was and what she was doing.

The inside of the home looked like a museum. Mom had an ability to put many different decors together and make it work. I remember her painting the rooms and moving furniture by herself when she was younger. There was always a stack of records. She played mariachi music as she cleaned the house. I believe that she was an artist. She showed me how to model with clay. I feel that much of my own artistic aspects come from her.

She could be very loving at one moment and shift, at least with me, in a heartbeat.

I believe much of her behavior was caused by constant trauma with Dad. She had no models for how to mother in a healthy way. Her discipline could be very harsh, although I have little recall of this. Both my older brothers remember and talk about having their ears bopped by her. They claim that this may have played a role in their hearing loss later.

I do remember being forced to kneel on the bathroom floor for hours. Even though I have no recollection of what I may have done to deserve this punishment, I can only assume it was relatively bad. We were sent, or at least I was sent, into our bathroom, and then told to bend down on our knees, on the old linoleum tile, for an extended period of time. It seemed to me that the time was set to when our father would come home, although I do not recall much of a consequence once he arrived. We were not supposed to squat down from our knees to our butts, but I know I did at times. For a long time I played this down, claiming that it only happened once.

I also went to school with electric cord welts on my butt and lower back. I showed them to no one. She could call me *mi rey* (Spanish for my prince or my king) and in the same sentence call me *cara de perro* or dog face.

She could come across very loving and then say terrible things. She said that the kids at school were going to laugh at me because I smelled like donkey urine because I was a bed-wetter. I did this with my own children, reinforcing that we were failures as parents because of our children's misbehaviors or mistakes. I know she believed that others would judge the family harshly as poor quality people. Some of the names she called me may have been terms of endearment, but most of them just confused the hell out of me. Much of what all of us have shared as a family is the art of sarcasm. Many times it is not what, but how you say it.

Mom was a great cook and made almost anything taste good, even when she wouldn't eat it herself. She worked very hard during the holidays and made dozens of tamales and other foods for the parties that would happen at our house. Many of these gatherings would end up with my parents fighting. She was deeply hurt by him. A couple of years before he died, most likely contemplating his mortality, he approached her and asked if she could ever forgive him. Without even raising her head she stated without hesitation, "NEVER."

Mom could be very contrasting. She did not want to go places with him, yet they traveled quite extensively. Wherever they went, she was loved by the new people they met. One of these times occurred in a timeshare that they used in Sedona. She did not want to go with the crowd, so she stayed close to the room. Apparently, she helped a couple who were from out of the country and did not know their way around. She showed them how to do what they needed despite the lack of verbal communication.

She could be a lot of fun and contrast that quickly. Alcohol was not her best friend and many times brought out the worst in her—something else we had in common. Like with the writing about my dad, I don't want to bash my mom. They were attracted to one another for a reason. Perhaps that reason was to bring their children into this world to make a difference. I am grateful that I have grown in forgiveness related to her. In my studies as to how all this came together, it is clear that she came from a place of great trauma, and the fact that she did as well as she did coming from that trauma, and that we as her children turned out as well as we have despite carrying much of the same energy, is amazing.

When I first started to study all this family-of-origin stuff, I happened to listen to a cassette tape in my truck. The lady speaking on the tape said, "We choose our parents," and went on to say more that I did not hear because I instantly reacted and quickly threw the tape out the window. My thought at that time was, "Why in the hell would I choose this shit?" Now I know that I could not be the person that I am becoming without those that I came from. Why have I chosen healing, expansion, forgiveness and a journey of self love? My response now is why not?

## Troy

I started grade school with tremendous fear. I was one of very few children of minority heritage. I started first grade the same way I graduated from high school: completely emotionally ill-prepared. I found myself in a group whose members were finding their place in the coming pecking order. One of these was a kid named Troy.

I believe that we were in a second or third grade class together. I have the class picture somewhere in my home. There we were, hands folded in our laps with all of our big heads that we had not grown into yet. Troy and I were not close in that group of boys who grew up together at that school. I was, it seemed to me, third behind the top guys who were the stars in sports, fights and, of course, with the girls.

Troy was on the fringes of the group. He was heavy and used that to be a bit of a clown, as a way to try to fit in. At the same time a popular TV program was The Jackie Gleason Show. He, too, was heavy, and part of his act was to exaggerate swiveling his hips. Troy would mimic this at school. There were times when as a group we would make him do this for amusement. It's funny that even way back then I did not feel good about this, most likely thinking of times I had been put on display for the family's amusement.

When I was around the age to be in 7th and 8th grades or junior high, around 1967-1968, some of the kids in my class created a rock band. It was the time of the Beatles, Rolling Stones, and The Doors. The group needed a place to play and practice so Troy, who was in the band, offered his house.

Troy's house had a huge living room, where the band used to practice until they let him go. In order to get in the side door, you had to squeeze by a large boat parked in the carport. The oleanders on that side of the house were so tall and huge they made a tunnel-like effect. I thought that was so impressive.

With grade school and junior high over, we moved on to high school where the distance between us grew. I had started using pot and experimenting and Troy was a drinker. His father was a real cowboy—he grew up ranching—so that influenced Troy. So in the beginning he was the cowboy hard drinker and I was the druggy hippy. We would talk every once in a while and he would put on this demeanor of the grown-up and warn me about the evils of drugs as he was literally falling down drunk.

His message had little influence. Troy had a pattern of demeaning himself with over-the-top displays of being drunk. He would fall down to get those around him to laugh. It was the same as the grade school stuff. As I study myself in this, I see that I played out most of my life in a perpetual state of serious. I would state often I was over forty-five years old most of my childhood and adolescence.

Troy and I had a few classes together in high school our last year. We again did not have much to do with one another; we ran with different groups. Our personalities were so different. I was somewhat serious and, I thought, more grown-up or mature. Looking back now it was more about being depressed. Troy's personality was more like a child. A case in point was when we were in a senior year human relationship class and he was throwing spit wads. It was very discomforting for me. Being around those who acted out in any form of childish or even childlike behaviors was not pleasant for me at all.

Within the high school experience, Troy and I began to overlap behaviors as he was introduced to pot and other substances, and I continued on my own planned or unplanned expansion in the same area. Our friendship was a natural fit for me even though we were from totally different realms of life. The one common denominator was the drinking and use of drugs.

Graduation was right around the corner, and a group of us radicals were getting together our own all-night party out in the desert, not connected to the school's planned graduation party. Although Troy was not one of the main players in getting it together, he did play a role in distributing directions and the time. We were to meet in the parking lot of the school with those who wanted to caravan. I had lined up one of my cousins to supply me with sufficient alcohol for this event.

Well, thinking there would be a group at the parking lot, I excitedly waited and only one car showed up. It was Troy. We waited and waited, but no one else showed. So we did the next best thing. His uncle had scored him some white lightning moonshine. Need I say more? So at some point we decided to head into the desert. I was somewhat disappointed that this was going to be a no-show for everybody I'd thought would show up.

By the time we got to the party spot, it looked like Woodstock. Cars were parked everywhere and somebody ran in front of my car naked followed by another and I knew I helped create something special. I recall very little of that night, but I remember that I was thinking that in the remote possibility that I was going to connect with a female there, my hopes would be dashed due to the fact I was incapable.

What I do remember was waking up in my car with a sheriff's officer tapping on my window with a night stick. I rolled down the window, and he asked me, "Do you know who that is? In the other car?" As I tried to focus, I glanced over and the only other car out there besides mine was Troy's. As we both got out to speak to the officer, I did not know what to say. Troy instantly told him, masterfully and with a cowboy accent, that after the graduation get-together, we realized we were too drunk to drive. I stood there in complete amazement at how he was so believable with the line of bullshit he was telling the officer, so successfully that the guy told us he was glad we chose not to drive. The truth is we were incapable of even walking, let alone driving. The officer started telling us about his graduation night, and then he let us go. I can look back now and see that was a pivotal point in our relationship. After twelve years of being around each other at a distances, Troy and I had finally found what we had in common: getting high.

I was very lost when I left school. After graduation, I started hanging out with Troy at his house. It worked out well that his parents let us drink even though we were under-age. I witnessed and experienced all kinds of trauma-related behaviors and was able to ignore much of it at the time. My understanding about the depths of that would come later. As I reflect back on that time and assess the energy of the environment, I can now see the great dysfunction that flowed through the house and through each one of us who were regulars here.

## Marriage

Joe the Barber was a friend of my father's. They had grown up together. When I needed a haircut, my father took me to Joe's place. I had a full head of curly, bushy hair. I would walk into Joe's with this bush of hair and walk out crying, with a buzz cut flat top. I never realized that we always left late to do this. Later I would put it together that we would be the last of his customers so they could walk across the street to the bar where they drank regularly.

During one of these visits Joe asked me my age. He then told me he had a daughter the same age and showed me a picture of her. I was not impressed at all.

There was a time in the high school years that I got into a deep state of depression due to much of what was happening at home with my parents and an adverse reaction to some drugs I had done. I had been helping an uncle who worked for my dad's company. I have always felt that he sensed what was going on in me, and that was the reason for a phone call from my aunt. She asked me if I would come to a group party with the youth group of their church and I responded with a gracious thank you, but no. She then instructed me to be ready in twenty minutes, and before I could negatively reply, she hung up. Reluctantly, I went. I had nothing in common with many of my cousins who were sure to be there. Did our family have anything to do with the church, any church?

I walked in and sat down next to a cousin who was my age, with the music of Lead Zeppelin playing. Within a very short time our conversation turned to drugs. I did not feel as out of place then. As we were talking, my eye caught a beautiful girl walking in with a guy who wasn't fit to be in her presence. Within a moment the guy just walked off. After gazing at her for a while and watching her meekly greet others who were there, I leaned over to my cousin and asked who she was. He said, "that's Joe [last name]'s daughter." That name meant nothing to me. Then he said, "Joe the barber's daughter."

The picture he had shown me years back did not do her justice. As I looked at her I could not understand why she would be with that classless guy, but he turned out to be her younger brother. At some point, I made my way to her and began a conversation with her. It was unlike myself to do this with any girl, much less someone this beautiful. People were starting to get thrown in the pool and she shared her reluctance to this as did I. She said she did not swim and I told her I did not believe in god, yet we met at this church group swimming party. Go figure. I thought she looked like a beautiful Indian princess.

My relationship with her grew. We went to different schools across town and, obviously, she lived near her school. I had gone to her home on occasion and reacquainted myself with her father whom I had not seen in years. It was obvious that I was done with the flat top hair cut as I walked into their house with shoulder-length hair.

We saw each other when we could, and she was one of the first people I went to shortly after my mother had attempted suicide, exposing much of my emotion related to that. We talked on the phone often.

During this period Troy's family had taken me in as one of their own sons. I considered his father my surrogate father, since I did have not much of a relationship with my own. I was planning to be married two weeks after my 20th birthday, and at that time Troy's family announced they were planning to move. So at 19 years of age, I was actually able to buy that house. A couple of years later, Troy bought the house next door to his own childhood house. It was a blast for years.

When my wife and I had first met those many years ago, we did not know that our families had known each other very well for many years. With our marriage we brought our own form of dysfunction into Troy's childhood home for another thirty years. Even though the dysfunction did not look the same, it still flowed in the house and in each one of us. We recreated many of the dynamics from our families.

We were young and I had lots of get-togethers where drinking and getting high were the pattern. Troy and some of the guys would come down and we would party, much to the dismay of my then wife.

Within a couple of years Troy would move back to Phoenix and move in with one of the gals of our group. Soon they were married and ended up buying the house next door. They had a child, a boy, and my wife and I had three children, a daughter and two sons. I thought this was great. Troy got into the fire department and I worked for my father for awhile, then eventually started my own company and became self-employed.

A couple of years went by and Troy got divorced. My wife and I stayed together but there was strain in the relationship due to the drinking and all the dysfunction that comes with it. Sometime after Troy's divorce a young lady moved in with him, and they would be together for 22 years. Her name is Susan.

When I went into treatment, I did not tell Troy or anyone else outside the family. I was actually afraid that he would have an adverse reaction to my choice to quit using. I had no idea how this might impact our friendship. Although Troy continued with the smoking of tobacco as well as the abuse of alcohol, he turned out to be quite supportive of my choice, at least when he was not drinking.

At one point, I went over to speak to the both of them. My purpose was to make amends for some behaviors that were disrespectful to the both of them, especially to Susan. I got very emotional as I left. A short time later I got a phone call; it was Troy. He asked if I was okay and then said, to my amazement, that he could not believe that I could do that, have the courage to admit my behavior and offer to make amends, then added he knew he could never do that.

Over the years, we would speak about my choice to quit and his to keep on using although only on occasion. I had at least one confrontation with him when he was trying to help my wife while I was gone. He was heavily under the influence and busted up some stuff at our house. I told him that I loved him as a brother, but he was not to come over while under the influence. I would be there for him if he wanted to let go of his drinking. He did not talk to me for months.

At some point we resumed talking. For awhile the four of us—Troy, Susan, my wife and I—started doing a few things together such as visits to cowboy art shows and a few baseball games. One time, it was just he and I who went. He did not drink at all and I told him with a lot of emotion that this was one of the best times we spent together.

After his first heart attack and while he was in the hospital, I talked to Troy one more time about his addictions. I had asked him what it was like to have the heart attack. He told me it was indescribable; he could not even attempt to describe the pain. There were tubes in every orifice of his body. I told him this, "Look, all the doctors are talking about is the smoking and nothing about the drinking. You and I are brothers and I will never bring this up after this, but if you choose to quit the alcohol I will be right there for you all the way." His response was, "How am I going to have fun?" My response back was, "Troy, look at yourself—you have tubes stuck everywhere in you. You could not even describe the pain you experienced. It does not look like you are having fun right now." I never said a word again.

I went on some hunting trips with Troy, but once I was in treatment, I had to back off due to what I saw with the drinking, mindset and behaviors that were affecting Troy negatively. As a matter of fact, I came back angry from the last hunting trip because of what I had seen, knowing there was nothing I could do about it. I even made a comment to someone that he was killing himself.

About six months later he was gone.

Although my wife and I had just separated, it would be my estranged wife who called me and told me that Troy went code in the White Mountains. I remember seeing him as he was getting ready for the trip. It was all I could do to not tell him, "God, you look like shit," but I did not say a word. The same week that my soon-to-be ex-wife moved out, Troy died of a broken heart.

The trauma that my wife and I had developed together would eventually guide each of us into recovery and guide me to my journey towards healing. Again it's interesting. It would have been easy to consider my marriage a failure, but I eventually saw it as part of the expansion of my healing: no one at fault, no one to blame.

## Powerful Children

Very early on I started to understand how family dynamics influence the futures of children, as it relates to when addiction is present. I believe this was something that surfaced while in treatment, or at least shortly after. I had purchased a number of books on understanding all the issues related to what was popularly called the dysfunctional family, or the alcoholic family system. The reality was I had some kind of knowing about this since I was a child.

The pervasive violence between my parents did not feel like anything right. At one point in one of these many conflicts—I don't know how old I was at that time—I got the courage to ask the question, and now I realize that asking the question at such a young age is confirmation that I knew this behavior was not right. "Why do you guys fight like this?" My mother's immediate response was "Everybody fights like this and you will fight like this, too."

I did not say a word, but inside my head was a resounding, "No way am I going to do this, at least not this way." What I have come to understand is that whatever was modeled to my mother as a child created a powerful perception and belief that she accepted as her truth. She then attracted a relationship that would model that perceived truth and, even though the emotional energy was toxic and destructive to all involved, it was still her truth. My father, given his history, attracted his own perception of a relationship.

My childhood statement inside my head, "No way would I do this," had some truth in it. I modeled dysfunction; however, I did not do it in exactly the same way. In my relationship with my wife, we rarely yelled and screamed; the destructive damage to things was not as pronounced. I cannot and will not say it never happened; it just was not as profound. In my head it seemed to be different from what was modeled to me. What was not different was the toxic energy that resonated in our home. Our children were absorbers of that energy, just as we were, just as our parents were and back and back and back.

What still amazes me is the ability and the power of children to create ways to survive these environments, even at the cost of giving that very power away. Those in the middle of trauma can leave their physical bodies to distance themselves from the pain. Yet that pain remains stored in that same body. One day it may be released and healed if those affected can let go of the emotional connection to that identity and to other traumas they may have gone through. All I can do is model that process to the best of my ability.

Here's an example of the power of what children can decide to do and think. While talking to one of my friends, he brought up something about his past. He shared with me that somehow he started fixating on evil. He said that his fear of evil was growing, until one day he made the decision *to be* evil. In that way he could reduce the fear. That decision affected him for years with obsessive thoughts, yet he never acted upon these thoughts. At the time his behaviors were coming close to acting out with evil, he left his hometown and went to a treatment center. This is where we met, and have been supporters of one another for almost 20 years. What is amazing to me is that two decisions, one as a child to choose evil and then another choice to not act out in evil, empowered him to alter what was becoming a very destructive life.

Another example involves the power of choice when a little girl decides not to have children. A friend had made this choice and as an adult came to question it. As she shared, not only about her last relationship, but also the ones previous, I could see a pattern. I believed that she was a powerful being due to some of her past experiences. While she was working through some of the grief and trauma she experienced, I told her, "You are a powerful woman."

She did not believe me, but I said, "In talking about your life and the relationships you have been in, I see a pattern that I believe gives evidence to your greatness. All the relationships you have attracted in your life have supported that powerful decision you made as a child to not have children. So even then you had the wisdom and a knowing. You attracted those who would support that power of the child. You already knew." How true is that for so many others? Perhaps even all of us.

**Emotional Detox** is the middle of the medicine wheel; the vortex of power is in the center. Oftentimes, we are focused on the outside, but the center holds the power. Our center, our power, is the heart chakra. It's the center of the healing circle, which represents the body and, in the center of the body, is the heart, lined up with all the chakras. Instead of living in the extremes, we can move to the center and use our hearts rather than our brains.

## The Table

My wife and I were young, in our early 20s, just married, and had bought our first home. Wow. It was 1973, the beginning of the decline of the hippie movement, yet I was a diehard.

The house we had bought from Troy's parents was almost totally furnished, but, little by little, we wanted to make it our own. As I said, I was a diehard, so it was important to decorate the house the right way. In the center of the living room we had a table made from a large electrical spool. It was covered with plants. The house was already blessed with yellow shag carpet and the macramé plant hangers and, oh yeah, the mattresses on the floor as couches. But my pride and joy was the beer tab curtain between the dining room and the kitchen; it didn't matter that as you brushed by it would grab and pull your hair out. No matter the sacrifice, it was really cool.

Of course, we had to have brass, from candle holders to wall art. One day while driving around, I saw a shop that advertised everything in brass. I stopped in to check it out. Once in, I looked around and in the process came across a claw-foot oak pedestal table. It was covered with all kinds of stuff: odds and ends. Liquid spills had dried over most of the surface, but it was in really good condition otherwise.

A guy came around from the back of the store. He looked like a crusty old cowboy. I asked if the table was for sale. He said, "Everything in this place is for sale." We talked about all the stuff in the shop, but I kept going back to the table. I finally made an offer which he countered. We did this for awhile and then he said, "This is what we will do: we will flip a coin. The winner gets his price, the loser buys a bottle of whiskey."

This was a win-win for me. So this table was blessed with a bottle of booze, as the two of us took our time, drinking until well after closing time. I had no way of knowing what would be experienced around this table in the following decades. A few days later, I put the table in my truck and brought it home. This was to be our first nice piece of furniture, but it needed some work. I set it in the house and began sanding it, no matter the mess. There was always an open can of beer or a drink not far away during this process.

So later we found some oak chairs to match and stained it all. It turned out great and became the the centerpiece of the home. We had no children yet and we were young with plenty of like-minded friends.

"Like-minded" meant mind-altered, so there were plenty of get-togethers. We were the first to be married and have our own place, and we had all been partying there before, so a natural flow of energy continued. My wife did not drink or use, so many times she was tired and more than likely frustrated with the activities. She'd go to bed and we would continue on around the table until the wee hours in the morning. As time passed, my using did not get better: undiagnosed and untreated, it never gets healed.

Time went on, and the gatherings diminished when many of those involved moved on with their own journeys. The table was still the center of our home and the activities around it expanded with us. So without the distractions of so many others to deflect, it was just us. I believed at the time that we were doing fine, or at least it was easy to see it that way. But tensions grew between us, and there were times when I would call and say—with all sincerity— that I would be home in an hour. By the time I got home a cold plate would be sitting on the table. When we did sit together at the table I wanted to talk, yet I could not come up with much.

Then my wife informed me that we were going to have our first child, our daughter. I was in total fear while trying hard to be the proud father-to-be. I knew deep within myself just how ill-prepared I was. Yet, god forbid, I would not show that to anyone. This feeling only expanded with the birth of our two sons. The dynamics around the table grew more toxic. My frustration expanded and my negative self-worth grew; both came out sideways as anger and judgment directed towards my family, yet I still tried hard to play the role of a healthy father figure. I was unaware that I had never had this modeled to me.

Then came the fatherly lectures to the children. The table became a false place of perfection. I always thought the children were well-behaved at restaurants; the truth was, they had been programmed at home not to make a mistake. Spilled milk or dropped food was a major deal. Later, as the kids grew, there were more fatherly lectures. My wife and I did the best we could, but we never worked together. I was trying to be an adult parent with nothing but an immature, wounded emotional state of being. I wanted so badly to feel like a secure, healthy, adult human. It was not going to happen.

My wife started looking for help, and the tension only grew. There would be another turning point around the table that I sensed had been coming for years. My behaviors were not only obvious to my wife, they were creeping into my own awareness. Then one day after a long day at work, I came home to the kids getting ready for something. When I asked what was going on, my wife said those dreaded four words, "We need to talk."

She said that my sister was coming to take the kids to her house. My body reacted with a familiar feeling of being overwhelmed. My defenses went up because I was in terror. She said that we would talk after the children were picked up. I said, "No, if you have something to say, say it now."

Just then my sister pulled up. Right before she entered the house, my wife looked at me and said, "David, you're sick, and you need help."

As I sat there at the table I heard somebody say, "I know" and to my amazement those words had come from me. "What do I do?"

Without any details of what was going on, my sister had responded to just the energy she felt through the phone when my wife asked her to please pick up the kids. She came inside, walked up to me, and saw and felt the pain radiating from me. With tears in her eyes she said to me, "I love you and everything is going to work out."

I was capable of only accepting half of the statement. I felt and totally accepted her love, but there was no way, in that moment, that anything was close to ever working out. It turned out we were both accurate; the way everything had been created in our home around that table was not going to work out, but something totally different would work out. It's taken many years to begin to grasp that reality. The experience of that day might have seemed in the moment to be the hardest to go through, yet it was an experience a few days later that I hope I never forget.

We were sitting all together, again at the table: my wife and the children and I. I wanted to tell them what was about to happen. I was going to an inpatient treatment center. I felt that it was time to be as honest as I could be.

This is the picture of what was happening as we sat together: I am speaking to ten-, eight- and seven-year-old children and my wife. "I am going to a hospital; they aren't going to cut me or anything like that. I think it is more like a school. They are going to help me stop drinking and I believe it will help me not be so angry so much." I know I must have said more yet I don't remember much. What I do recall was looking at each one of them.

My wife was crying; she had been praying for this moment for years, so I could understand her emotion. My daughter—who is very intuitive and sensitive–was also crying. Then our oldest son, also very sensitive, began to cry.

But it was our youngest son who moved me. He had already put up a protection around himself not to feel, yet he was crying also. I knew that the energy of our family was shifting and something powerful was happening around that table.

At that table many years later, my wife and I would decide to be divorced after thirty years together. Shortly after she moved out, my close childhood friend made his transition to the Source. I began to share whatever I could related to my own healing with his widow, offering her support with many conversations—again around the table. A couple of years later we would become a couple. Susan has been one of my greatest teachers. As I look back to all that has happened around that table and how I am now open to all coming possibilities, I am amazed.

I don't think I'll ever let that table go.

The table – in David's kitchen

# HEALING

## The Treatment Center

Having been confronted about my lifestyle—or maybe a more relevant term would have been my deathstyle—I entered treatment. The days before were emotionally traumatizing. I could not have ever conceived that I would be doing this. My primary motivation was to salvage the relationship with my wife and children. While I could concieve that it might be slightly possible to not drink, there was no way I could live without being in that relationship. My willingness to enter treatment was also because I believed it validated that, at my core, I was broken and flawed and defective, so weak that everyone was right about me being a poor excuse of what a real man is supposed to be.

The whole family drove to the treatment center, and we went in together. When it came time for them to leave, you would have thought I was on a suicide mission destined never to return. Oddly enough, there would be much more truth in this than I could ever imagine.

When they left me there, I had no idea what to expect. I did not know if I would witness the horrible detox of others already there. I walked around, did my best to avoid everybody, and made my way over to a large chalkboard covered with writing. One statement caused me much discomfort, a quote from Jimmy Buffet. "We are the people our parents warned us about." What the hell had I done?

Inside the treatment center a large, central room held couches and chairs. Beyond that a group of people sat in a dining area with tables and chairs and a refrigerator. To my amazement, these people were laughing. I could not believe anyone could be happy or laughing in a setting like this. I was so full of shame.

Later that evening, nurses checked our blood pressure and other vitals. We were asked to come to the central room for some kind of talk. It turned out to be a person from outside the center who volunteered to speak to the new people. As he started out, I don't know if I grasped what he was saying. One thing I did get:

that my drinking was not the whole reason for my being there. I had a strange sense about that; it seemed to set in motion the premise that, for me, this was not going be about a single substance, or at some point it would not even be narrowed down to abusing substances.

Later, I looked up *addict* in the dictionary. The definition I found opened up a new realm for me in my awareness related to recovery. I could not tell you anything that guy said, yet I know at my core what I thought I heard. This is it:

> "You are not the person you
> were when you were using and
> you are not the person you are
> capable of being."

I assume he thought this statement would feel warm and fuzzy or possibly encouraging. My reaction, starting from the top of my head and washing down my entire body, was an electric current of terror. I broke into a sweat. This was not by any means an unfamiliar emotional experience. I have experienced this sense of terror many times in my life.

The awareness I got from that statement, which he may or may not have said, but is what I chose to hear, was this: *I had no idea who I was*. I drank and used many things outside myself for about twenty years in order to *not* know what I perceived myself to be. Shortly thereafter I would realize that my using and drinking for that length of time served to keep me from remembering most of my first thirteen years. Hey, it worked! This statement was going to be the basis of what I was going to talk about for over twenty-five years: *Emotional Detox, Redefining Self* .

> **Emotional Detox** is about redefining our identity: our beliefs, emotions, and behavior. It's about redefining everything we thought we knew about ourselves. We are re-creating a new truth. It's about telling ourselves we want to turn the question, "What's wrong with me?" into the statement, "This is what's right with me."

Eventually I came to understand that toxic biochemical reaction, terror and sweating, was the release of energy stored in my body. I had created an identity in order to survive. If I let go of my terror, of my resistance to letting go, *then who am I?* It was the only identity I knew. Emotional Detox is about finding the courage to let go of the toxic, survival-self and re-create and co-create a *new* self, or reclaim the *true* self.

## Finding Happy

When I was in treatment, I started to reflect back to my introduction to drinking and drugs. An interesting awareness came up for me. I was in a place where I could, maybe for the first time, really look at my personal relationship with using substances to feel different. Alcohol was always present in my home. As a child I did not have any comprehension of what it represented to me; it was a normal part of the family system. Now I can look deeper to the energy about alcohol in that system. While there seemed to be some joy or fun connected to it, there was also a deep feeling of anger/rage as well as a depressed energy that reigned thoughout the house.

I now wonder if that was emitting from me. As I write this, I have an image of two characters from the cartoon *Peanuts*: Linus, who like I did, carried a blanket, and sucked his thumb and Pigpen. Like Pigpen, who had a cloud of dust that floated around him, there was a cloud of *sad and pissed* that surrounded me. Of course, I was unaware of this at the time; it was just what it was.

The whole drug thing seemed to have a different energy about it. I was a little older when I started using, yet young enough to not really get it. I don't really remember any real campaigns to educate about drugs. It was not "Just say no" or "This is your brain on drugs." The message to discourage us at that time, if anything, was the image of some scruffy guy standing just inside an alley, wearing a trench coat. As some kid would walk by, he would open up his coat— decked from top to bottom on both sides, the inside of the coat was lined with an assortment of drugs and all the paraphernalia. He'd say, "Hey kid, want some candy?" It was just enough to get a kid at least started using and possibly eventually to start his own business.

This was not what happened with me. I was maybe 11 or 12 years old, and my best friend and I were playing outside during the summer vacation. It was a warm evening and we were playing a little game that if a car drove down our street and the lights hit us, it would kill us. His older brother and his friend approached from down the street, laughing out loud hysterically. As they got closer I could feel my attraction to them. I wanted to know what was going on. I watched them for a while. When they were close enough so that I could ask them, they said that they had been doing grass.

I remember thinking, "Well, I have been rolling in grass all evening. All I felt was itching and sweaty." Then they said they had been smoking marijuana. I had no idea what they were talking about. But some 20 years later in a treatment center, the dots started to connect and the puzzle pieces began to fit together. I was struck with this powerful thought: what was my emotional reality then and before that I was so drawn to wanting what *looked like* happy pouring out of these guys? I now understand my statement that I used drugs and alcohol for 20 years in order to not deal with what my life felt like for the first 12 or 13 years. It was not long after my encounter with the laughing pot-smokers that I began trying to find *happy*.

### Treatment University

So now the education for me began. I had gone into treatment on a late Thursday afternoon, and not much happened with the exception of that first outside speaker. I walked around trying my best to avoid any of those I perceived as clients. I was deeply emotional. I walked up to a staff station and asked a woman what I could do or what was I supposed to do. She reassured me that the process would go forward, to be patient. I know she felt my anxiety. She reached into the desk and handed me some pamphlets related to Alcoholics Anonymous. I tried to read through them. I wondered why I was pressing so hard to find out I was supposed to do. It occurred to me that *what needed to be done* while there in treatment was more important. I had never seen myself as a very good student in school or most anywhere and, for the most part, barely got by. It was not for a lack of effort; I just seemed to not get it. Now, managing to look back, I can have a more expanded view of what was going on around me and more profoundly, what was going on within me.

So the initial thought was, "I will cram for the test, I will find out all the information early, then study, study, study. Perhaps this time I will get beyond the grading curve to a higher level. I will go beyond just 'slightly above average'." So I received the pamphlets yet I was totally incapable of seeing anything other than fine black lines on white paper.

One brochure was a bi-fold form laminated in plastic, the size of a business card. Printed on it was the Alcoholics Anonymous Twelve Steps and all related information. I glanced through it, then placed it in my wallet. I have never considered myself to be a superstitious person, not then and not now. Yet to this moment I have now carried that with me for over 26 years. I may have pulled it out and looked at it two or three times over the years. It has tattered edges where the paper is crumbling though the hazed and scuffed plastic laminate. It strikes me as odd that I have done this, but then this whole process is odd and this just fits right in.

The next couple of days I started interacting with some of the other clients. Still, it was nothing structured because it was the weekend. At some point my anxiety was sky high. I asked a lady psychiatric technician if I could please talk to her. Small, private offices surrounded the central meeting room, and she took me into one.

With a lot of emotional energy, I started explaining my frustration about not knowing what I was supposed to do. The more I talked, the more energy poured out of me. "What the hell is going on? I need to go to a class or to be assigned somewhere! It looks like others are going places." When I realized I was nearly screaming at her, I abruptly apologized and told her I did not mean to look as though I was angry at her. I just wanted to go forward with whatever the process was. She looked confused, which added to my own confusion. She told me not to be concerned with her feelings. She said, "I am a little surprised. Most people have this much energy toward wanting to get out, or convincing themselves that they don't belong here. It's refreshing to see someone with this much intensity about knowing what to do."

Shortly thereafter, I was assigned to a therapist, Sam, and a group. I moved to another part of the treatment center. As soon as I got to the group sessions, I heard one of the clients sharing his using story. I asked Sam when I could share mine. I think the first time his response was to say, "David, you have only been here a few hours, hold on."

They gave me an assignment to write out what my life was like after I started drinking and eventually using drugs. So to be ahead of it all, I started writing, yet something seemed to be missing. I didn't know what it was until I heard others' stories. We were asked to write about things we remembered from the age of 0 to 5 years old. I had always felt that nobody could have any memories of this early time of his life. So I had nothing to write and in my head was this: "No matter where I was, I was in the way and somehow where I was, I was not supposed to be."

This last statement would become a very powerful awakening for me many years later on my path of healing. *I was not supposed to be!* When I tried to remember my life from 5 to 10 years old, that bio-chemical reaction started on the top of my head, moved slowly through my body. I did not remember large parts of my life, but I remembered the fights between my parents. Fights that would last for months at a time. I remembered the terror of starting school knowing that somehow I was totally ill prepared. I remembered that I was a bedwetter, but mostly I remembered the fights.

Then I remembered from 10 to 15 years: the fights, some parties and weddings, funerals, some camping trips. I also know this was the time frame when I started to use alcohol and drugs. The chemical reaction in my body grew stronger. There seemed to be so much I had little or no recall about. I have seen myself on 8 mm home movies, can see myself in them, yet to this day I have no tactile emotional experience of being there. So if the question was at what age could I first identify trauma, the only time or age would have been *in utero*.

My treatment center experience brought the realization that drinking alcohol, using drugs, or the multitude of things we do outside ourselves, are done in order to cope with what's going on inside. I was beginning to see clearly that this treatment center was really a university. It was about the most important subject on this planet: the fusing of my humanity and my divinity. It was about my SELF and my journey to be whole.

### Redefining Addiction

*Addiction*, n.: the process by which a person gives oneself up to a powerful habit, to be or become habitual, to devote or surrender oneself to something habitually or obsessively.

I was interested in the definitions of the term *addict*. I started looking up words and found many of them to mean something different than I had believed them to mean. I had issues related to the powerlessness that seemed to be so much of my introduction to recovery. It was not much of a stretch for me to own that my life, my health, and my relationships with my wife and children, were in deep decline. Emotionally, I was broken.

So the powerlessness concept made sense, yet there was something I was resistant to about owning it for the rest of my life. I admit that this may not be what the Twelve Steps is all about, but it was how I perceived it. I started to look at the wording that defined an addict. I was first drawn to the terms, *to give oneself up or to devote/surrender oneself to*. I started to see a deeper meaning. Was I powerless or was I giving my power away? Surrendering it? If this was what I was doing, then why or how?

When I started my process of healing, it was based on a very limited understanding of alcoholism and addiction. When I walked into the treatment center in Phoenix, Arizona, it was not my desire really to stop drinking. I wanted to keep the relationship with my then wife, and I wanted to resolve my relationship with my young children.

Given my emotional and mental state, my perceptions and beliefs really brought me to that moment. It is obvious to me now, looking back to that day, that my self-loathing proceeded to my decision to walk into this place called treatment, which turned out to be a university. I wonder, given the state of emotional discord I seemed to be in at that time, why it was not suggested that an intake to the psych ward would have been more appropriate. It would have validated just how broken and weak-minded I was.

So I share this little bit of what was going on within me as evidence that there were some really strong self-esteem issues going on. I was horribly hard on myself, something I have made much powerful progress with, yet it is still a challenge at times even now. In some way I knew on some level that I did not need to be reminded of just how defective I was. I had expected that to be a part of what I would receive while in treatment. I am grateful that did not happen. Instead I was educated about how this was created within me and around me. I began to see the science in this, that I was a part of the dysfunction. Not wholly of the dysfunction, but just a part of it. This allowed me to grasp for the first time that it may not be all my fault.

I was willing to take responsibility for my part. I thought I knew what to expect. I was not going to be surprised if I were to be pounded with this great moral lesson, exposing my imperfections. But it turned out that I did not need anyone to kick me while I was down; I was very good at doing that to myself all by myself. I was made aware that through certain filters I can interpret information and have feelings and reactions about that information. This relates to the first speaker I heard. I am not sure what he said, but I know what I heard.

It became clear that this was part of a long pattern going back to before the time I started drinking or using. Addiction was a learned behavior that allowed me to survive. The next word I looked deeply into was *oneself:* one's normal, healthy, or sane condition or self. My way to describe my one self is that part that is whole, or wholly. I have said it this way when I am blessed as I am doing my talks. My journey is about bringing together the *self*, my humanity, with *SELF*, my divinity.

The next words that called to me were *be* or *being*. My next powerful awareness related to these words in the the context of defining addiction was related to that first night in treatment. This was when I was in total terror due to the fact I was faced with not having any concept of who I was. All my survival behaviors and all the habits I used to get through the traumas in my life had created an identity, an identity I obviously had great disdain for and disgust with or I would not have tried so hard to numb it and slowly torture it toward death.

Yet I did not have any idea of this at the time, and it was the only identity I knew. My fear was that if I let it go, who would I be? I heard a term that modeled my healing: "It is a good day to die." It has been Hollywoodized to depict only a brave warrior going out to battle with the honor of possible death. That's one version, but there is another. It is the death of the old identity that no longer serves. It is the letting go of the old self to be reborn or renewed to the true self. It is the ultimate spiritual journey.

I was confused by the deep emotional grieving process of letting this old self go, even though it was destroying me and hurting many of those around me.

But even though it has been a long process filled with resistance, I can say that I have made major progress in the process of transformation. I have been very dedicated to my journey into healing. There is a Native American metaphor related to this process. It is the virgin birth, the spiritual awakening within each one who chooses rebirth.

The redefining of the term addiction opened up many other aspects that are not directed towards substance alone. My definition of addiction became using anything outside of myself to numb or alter my insides. This opens up many ways of understanding an expanded view of addiction. I began to look at events that impacted me that would not ordinarily have been placed in the box called *addiction*. I recognized one of the most destructive symptoms of addiction is racism. Not only the racism between races, but the racism within races. Statements that demonstrate this are: "Well, if this group were not here then somehow I would feel better or safer," or "if these people would only go back to where they come from."

I have wanted to carry a large photograph of the earth from a satellite beyond Saturn that shows the fuzzy blue dot that is our planet. I'd like to show it to whomever would make this request of me and tell him or her, "This is were I come from." We all actually originate in the space that surrounds our Earth and expands throughout the universe. That's an even larger concept that would be worth the investment of a lot more energy and contemplation.

So now we move on to another aspect of redefining. Through my healing, I involved myself in many modalities to find out how I created myself and get some understanding of the great emotional pain I had experienced. At one place I went to, they spoke of two concepts that affected me very much. One was *cause and effect,* which I understood to be related to my history. The other would bring a very powerful awareness to me. This was simply the concept of *I AM.*

The treatment center used the Twelve Steps as a support to what they were teaching. The first time I heard the affirmation of the first step, "We admitted we were powerless over alcohol—that our lives had become unmanageable," I thought to myself, "Well, duh." I had expected to hear more than the obvious.

Again, I own this is through my own filters. I had a reaction to words like *powerless, character defect* and others. The whole aspect of god and *higher power* also triggered something inside me. I only saw a little of this concept modeled in my home when trauma was ramped up. Now I see that my connection to god or prayer was with the toxic energy in my home environment. Another aspect was that I was going to be judged for moral reasons. What began to help me with this was my attraction to the science or physics of the whole of behavioral health. The idea of *cause and effect* was one of first concepts that intrigued me. Could it be that we are effects? And if we can understand the cause, we can change the effect?

I felt empowered by that possibility. I began to understand that we are bio-chemical electrical systems and that one of those energies in motion is *emotion*. Understanding this can allow some of us to not judge this energy as good or bad, or to have to suppress it, but allow it to move through us, allow an *Emotional Detox*. Thoughts, perceptions and beliefs are creative energies that can be healing or can create dis-ease. It is by understanding the power of the spoken word that we co-create with this, as well; memories are stored in every cell of our bodies, and we constantly replace those cells with new cells.

This question was asked of me once: If we are constantly replacing old cells with brand new cells, then why do we still create dis-eases? I believe it is because we are infusing the new cells with the same old energy, thus reinforcing the stronger cell based in the old perception and beliefs. Thus we create a stronger cell base in dis-ease. Or we can choose to infuse the new cells with new thoughts, perceptions, and beliefs, and we can then move into a deeper level of healing, overcoming or replacing dis-ease.

I realized that early in my life it had been important for me to give up my power. It took me some time to understand this, but I had given my power away in order to survive, and it worked. But these old survival techniques played hell with my ability to have healthy relationships, most importantly my relationship with myself and my connection with Spirit.

Going through the Emotional Detox of the identity I had created in the past, and allowing myself to input new thoughts that challenged my old perceptions and created new beliefs moved me into healing and away from the dis-ease I had actually become. It was who I used be be. I know that statement will connect with a certain percentage of those who have been attracted to this message. I have no idea what that percentage will be. I also know that for another percentage there will be no connection. Again, I do not know that percentage, either. It is not for me to know. It is for my *own* healing that I am writing this. I am dedicated to going forward in my expanded healing and to radiating that energy. I know that will affect others—how, again, is not for me to know.

At the spiritual center that I attended in the beginning of my journey, I was very drawn to the physics of light. It was mentioned that light could be measured both as a particle and as a wave, that it was a form of matter as well as it is energy. I began to understand and accept that we are all bio-chemical electrical systems, and that we are also both particle and wave. I understood that we are energy. I began to own this and it started to help me take responsibility for how I used that energy: thought, belief, perception was all energy. I could understand that long-embedded perceptions that I accepted as truth had created a reality that was not totally of my own making. I had taken on from others the energy I was surrounded with through most of my early life, and unknowingly made it my own.

My path has led me to owning my part in the recreation of energy that has not served me for most of my life. It is now my responsibility to let go of not only the behaviors, but to let go of the emotional attachment and the identity that was also created.

I began speaking at a treatment center to clients in the early stages of recovery from addiction. I asked them to consider this possibility: there is a cause that has created this effect and we are the effect. At least part of this is our behavior. There is no one at fault or no one to blame. That does not mean that we don't have to take responsibility. We have accountability for those that we may have affected in a negative way, including ourselves.

My repetitive thoughts had created a belief, deeply influenced by perception. This supported my behavior, to which I had an emotional attachment. The powerful self-identity increases all of this. Perception and emotional attachment have been major elements of my own healing transformation. For many years, I had no clear idea of how this was affecting me, only that the emotions were many times overwhelming because I did not realize the resistance I had to letting go of the only identity I knew. Hence, I held on to emotional energy related to that old self.

Confused by my overwhelming emotions, I wondered at times if I was having a massive breakdown. I have always judged myself harshly, but an idea occurred to me early on while I was in the treatment center. If there was a biological and physiological chemical release from the body called detox, *then could there be a biological chemical detox equally as powerful on an emotional level?*

I shared this concept, and found people understanding it and relating to the concept. But even if they had not, it seemed to be a very important concept for me. So, in those early sessions in the treatment center, was I having a break*down* or a break*out*? I believe I was finally releasing all the toxic energy that I had carried throughout my life. I initially judged this process of being overwhelmed as bad and wrong. I had plenty of outside support that there was plenty wrong with me. But I now know that for me the process has been a gift for my healing and a gift to others as it allows me to model this path towards self-love.

I now look at the whole relapse/suicide choice in a different way. Does relapse mean going back to using unhealthy and destructive behaviors to attempt to numb out the Emotional Detox pain rather than going through the discomfort of healing? Or is it caused by the fear of letting go of the old identity even though it no longer serves? Could suicide be the murder of the wrong self-identity?

I have been blessed with the ability to look back on the path I have chosen to walk. I know that I have had many good days to die on that path. I now see clearly that the many times I considered killing myself, I would have been killing the many false identities I had created to survive.

I hated many of the clichés that were introduced to me in my early journey towards healing. It would really piss me off when I would walk up to some one and greet him with "It's good to see you," and that guy responds with "Well, it's good to be seen." I would say back, "How is it going?" and his response might be "Well, one day at a time." I'd say, "I heard you were going through some things," and his response might be, "Well, by the grace of god." So I might then say, "What the hell's wrong with you, can't you be real and have a conversation?!!!" His response: "Keep coming back." Me: *AAAAHHHH!!!!* Yet there is one cliché out of the many that has particularly affected and moved me: "Don't quit before the miracle." I have not quit and the miracle called SELF continues to expand like the universe I live in.

### Redefining everything I thought I knew

As I continued to listen and be open to what lessons there were for me to utilize in the understanding of cause and effect in my life, certain words and terms that I heard moved me in many ways. I was in a group when a reference was made to a particular word. I chose to look it up as I was beginning to use it in my own talks. The word was *sarcasm*: to tear flesh, bite, to cut; a sharp and often satirical or ironic utterance designed to cut or give pain; bitter, caustic and often ironic language that is usually directed against an individual.

So what was the connection I was having with this word? I started to look back at the interaction I have had with each of the members of my family. I realized I had created an illusion related to my family. I always believed, when we were together, that we were funny and cute; it seemed like that to me: there was always laughter. Yet the feelings did not always match the ripping into one another, tearing the flesh with words, and feeling the need to cover the discomfort with a chuckle. It was somewhat confusing for me. I started to see the family dynamics differently. I had a family that I had created and interpreted to be the way I wanted it to be. I was beginning to grieve the loss of that illusion. The pain of that was not any less than the grieving of any other loss that would more likely be considered to be reality.

This amazed me. So where else could this appear in my life. Would all those whom I attracted in my life have to fit this same pattern? I grieved the loss of friends I really never had. Given the law of attraction and the familiarity with where I came from, how could it not have been the same with most aspects of my life?

So then, little by little, I was exposed to the many elements in my life that I needed to redefine. Reluctantly and with resistance, I started with me. What had I created about myself that was based in the same illusion as my family and the people I had attracted to my life? I was starting to question every thing I thought I knew. What is *love*? What is *relationship*? What is it to be a man and a father? These and many more questions came to the surface. Most of my awareness did not begin with the complete answer. I may never come up with final definitions.

I started with recognizing what was not defined. I told others that in our marriage, my wife and I were close and we communicated well, we were happy and in love. I was totally convincing, I was very sincere, yet it was only half of the opinion. She had a much different view. So as I started to redefine everything, I looked at the relationship. I started to own the fact that I was more addicted to the relationship than to substance.

Now looking back at any relationship I've had, I would describe it like this: two separate half-people coming together in enmeshment to create a whole person. Hey, they wrote great love songs based on this theme. I used to listen to those songs and think how great it was that I was in that kind of relationship. I hear those same songs today and think how sick and co-dependent they are. Yet that is what I helped to create: a toxic co-dependent enmeshed union. And I called it *love*. How could I have done anything differently, given what I brought into the relationship, given all the beliefs and perceptions I created based on what I was familiar with—given my history?

Other words would soon cause me to wonder. At one time, after I had left the treatment center but was continuing with my own quest for healing, I was supporting a close friend. Susan had just lost the person she had been in a relationship with for over 20 years, and he had been a childhood friend of mine since first grade, and we then lived next door to each other.

I recall a conversation we had about our most recent relationships. They, in many ways, mirrored one another. They had ended at the same time, mine due to divorce, hers due to Troy's death. We both spoke about how much we cared for those in our past relationships.

For some reason the word *care* touched something inside me. Shorty after our talk I looked up the word *care*. Like so many things I thought I knew, the definition of this word was not at all what I thought. *Care*: 1. Suffering of mind: grief, a disquieted state of blended uncertainty, apprehension, and responsibility; a cause for much anxiety; painstaking or watchful attention.

I remember seeing on television, as a child, the news of a huge ship with *CARE* painted in giant red letters on its side. It was about a humanitarian act or medical help to impoverished people around the word. One definition of the word care represents this action. *Care*: 2. To feel trouble or anxiety; to feel interest or concern; to have liking, fondness, or taste. Yet the first definition most likely represented my personal emotional reality. Redefining it required going back to the story of my father. Was I having compassion or concern? The truth for me was that I was actually *carrying* others' emotional stuff and then somehow making it totally my own.

Understanding this has allowed me to begin separating my own care from that of others. It has been and continues to be an interesting process, but knowing this also allows me to take responsibly for myself. There is no one to blame or any one at fault. For me, that is what this path of healing is all about.

There are so many examples of redefining. Some can be very disturbing. Here is a case in point. I had a guy pass through my life years ago, and he made a comment about hating god. We had very similar environments growing up and had attracted similar relationships. We had the opportunity to study the dynamics of how we recreated this throughout our lives. I asked him a few questions.

First I asked: given what we have learned and what we were beginning to accept, just how different are our current beliefs and perceptions from what we had accepted as truth? We continued our conversations and I asked him what he thought of the concept of how he saw his family in the past and how he saw it now, given what he has accepted and how he perceived it now.

I asked him, "Can you admit that the way you saw your family was really inaccurate?" He said yes. Then I asked about his relationship with his wife. "Given what you know now, do you feel that the way you accepted that relationship in the past was inaccurate?" He said yes. Again the question was, "How do think about the way you view yourself now, rather than what you did from the past? Could it be that this was based on a false perception?" His response was a reluctant yes. So, I asked, "Okay, if all these perceptions from your past are so constantly not representative of the truth as you see it to be now, then could it be that your concept of god is also just as inaccurate? How could all these other perceptions and beliefs be so far off yet your concept of god be right on? Maybe you are using up energy by hating something that does not even exist."

Having this talk with this man gave me the opportunity to take responsibility for redefining my concept of god just as I had redefined all those other things I once thought I knew.

## Emotions

When I started this whole process of rediscovering my SELF, my emotions were overwhelming. So my emotions were much of the focus of what I expressed when I shared. These emotions were always part of my young life. They showed up very early in my life as uncontrollable rage, acted out in tantrums. I have no really clear memories of this; I know this because I was a topic of conversation within the family and a source of jokes at larger gatherings. They spoke about my head banging inside my crib and against walls. The cure for me, according to what my mother stated at some of these family gatherings, was to smack my head on the floor. Whether or not they meant to express that I was somehow defective, that there was something wrong with me, that was how I interpreted it.

I turned that rage inside in order to cope and created an alternative symptom called depression. Bedwetting was another aspect of this acting out. I have had a very difficult time with understanding emotions, and how to identify them in the context of healing. The most difficult one was to define *good* or *happy*, or what would be defined by some as *positive*. It is something I tried to create in the use of substances, relationships, and a multitude of things outside myself. The emotion releasing from me was so huge and so intense, it was not uncommon for this release to create an overload that would cause me to pass out.

Extreme anxiety and panic, which are nothing more than expressions of fear, caused this extreme desire for my body to shut down. That added to my perception that I was broken, flawed and somehow defective. In my healing I dedicated myself to letting go of this identification of a false self. It still amazes me just how much resistance I have had to this over the years but, after all, this had been the only self I had ever known, and the law of attraction had surrounded me with those who supported this self-identification.

*It's interesting* is a very common statement that is often made while speaking with those whom I feel blessed to have supporting me on my journey. It comes up as we share our process to transform the way we see the world and how we see ourselves in it. I am sometimes amazed how I have managed to attract these souls who support me. Then I reflect back and realize that I have always attracted them.

Years ago, when I first heard of the concept of the law of attraction, it came across to me as some woo woo new-agey concept. Yet as I continued to search out more knowledge that could put things together for me, it become clear that we all attract, all the time, whether we are aware or not, beginning with the influence of my family environment and the role I played within that system. It seemed in many ways I played a similar role with the group of kids I went to grade school with. I was not totally powerless over the entire group; I found a few that I could express some power over.

It may have looked on the surface as children just being children, but I now wonder if we were finding our position within the group. It's about finding who we will give power up to, and whom we could take power from. *It's interesting.* I grew up with this group of kids and some of us chose to act out in our behavior or, for some of us, by beginning to use alcohol and drugs. Those who did not partake dropped away. Sometimes I had a heavy judgment of them. It is not difficult to study our group and see many of us came from the same family dynamics . . . the law of attraction.

**Emotional Detox** is the release of energies that no longer serve, although they served at one time. When Emotional Detox happens, a new set of beliefs and, therefore, a new identity is created, co-created, and re-created. It's like rebirth, the Phoenix coming from the ashes.

As I got older and new people came into my life, all were similar in what we connected with. I did not hang out with those who did not drink or use. I can look back and recall just how limited the conversations were.

When I began to study all this as a part of healing, I was convinced that these powerful emotions were causing me to experience equally powerful thoughts. As I was introduced into the physics of energy that flows within me, I became aware of the power of thought. I chose to accept that the beginning of everything is thought. I had heard that in the beginning there was the word. The Bible says, "Let there be light," yet there had to be first the thought, *then* the word, and *then* the expansion of the universe (light).

*My attachment to my emotions was strong, but I felt an equal intensity and attachment to my healing. This was the creation of the concept of Emotional Detox.*

I believed that there was some validity to the Emotional Detox concept, yet I have to admit that in the power of the spoken word I was most likely keeping myself somewhat stuck in the emotions that were so much of my self identity. Yet as I continued to learn more about cause and effect, the concept was, little by little, shifting my understanding. So I continued to study, and for me it was most important to speak of how I was beginning to connect the dots.

Whether triggered by work, money or the biggest—relationships—, my pattern of reaction to emotions was an overwhelming need to do something. On the other side of that was the need to not do something. I can see now, looking back, the desire was to somehow alter the feelings. I thought I was judging the emotions as bad, but now I know I was the judging *myself* as bad. I did not know how to separate what I was emotionally releasing with how I defined myself. So if I felt bad it was because I *was* bad, or I would not feel this way.

This was happening at a time when I had chosen to stop altering these emotions with alcohol or drugs. I still did not want to feel this purge. It did not take long to realize that my way to manage feelings was to use. If this was what I was carrying within me from my childhood, no wonder I used. It was a way to survive and it worked, Yet it was no way to create healthy relationships, especially my relationship and my connection to my self and my connection to spirit.

## Judgment

---

**Emotional Detox** is letting go of moral judgment. We all judge. We judge our thought processes - we make a moral judgment. "I'm a bad person." "I'm weak." These judgments are inappropriate. If we use judgment to put somebody down or to get somebody to feel small, even ourselves, then it is a substance, a substance we are abusing the same as we might abuse alcohol or drugs. I learned how to judge as a kid. It's not a position of neutrality.

---

The more I shared and studied, it became clear that this was an important aspect for me to understand in a different way, to redefine this in another way. One of the first terms that I heard from a Science of Mind learning center was the concept of cause and effect. I started to wonder if I was part of an effect and shared this with others. If this was accurate, when we realize we don't like the effect, we can change. The change might be to redefine the emotions that are being released as part of the transformation, thus beginning to redefine ourselves. So I started to break it down like this: a repetitive thought creates a belief that is attached to a powerful perception supported by behavior. Data in the computer, data out.

If there is an emotional attachment to the belief and perception, then there is a powerful self identity to all. As I shared this with others, I seemed to make connections. I would have loved making this concept known to myself; this would have been the completion of the emotional discomfort.

As I stated earlier, it still amazes me just how much resistance there has been on my part. It is happening in increments. I am understanding more and more of what it takes to move beyond the causes. Some of it, in the beginning, is about redefining all that I thought I knew, yet it also takes more. For me, it is taking *judgment* out of the process.

I was a very sensitive child. My emotions ranged from rage-fueled tantrums to the complete silence of depression, and everything in between. Much of my journey has been wanting to have some kind of clarity about all this. I felt flawed, defective, and somehow broken. Understanding the physics of how things work has helped me significantly to understand and overcome. As my healing continues, more comes to me that helps me gain a better understanding, allowing me to let go of many of the negative self judgments that I have carried within me most of my life.

I would have thought it was about negative judgment. The reality is it is *any* judgment. It is about the tremendous amount of energy spent to fix something that most likely is not broken. This has played out a lot in wanting to fix others and even wanting to fix myself. As I become more accepting of my divinity and letting go of disgust toward my humanity, the more I move into acceptance of the moment by letting go of the resistance. It is to move into the art of just allowing with trust and faith that I can accept all the abundance that the universe has to offer.

I am still a work in progress. I still wonder if I even come close to representing the path of healing and transformation to the life I want. When I started on this path toward healing, I wanted to understand the process. But in striving for that understanding, I do not want to forget that what I desire most of all is to embrace peace and calm within me and not judge the contrast as being other that what it is: part of the process.

### Divinity and Humanity

Over the years I experienced many examples of the *divinity* and *humanity* without really getting the true tactile understanding of what it would mean for my future healing path.

The minister at a spiritual learning center that I attended years ago was tremendously talented in simplifying complicated aspects—at least complicated for me—of teachings related to Religious Science. She was gifted with the ability to be well prepared and spoke with little or no notes. She was a powerful speaker and teacher. Yet, I heard mutterings from others about how she conducted the center's business. Another man I knew, who held a doctorate and taught the science of unique healing processes, was criticized by someone who had done some work for him.

When these healers were doing their art, I perceived them as radiating their divinity. It was easy for me to watch and listen to these gifted teachers. When they were "in the zone," I knew they had tapped into the channeling of spirit. Had I the ability, I know I would have seen white light radiating into them and from them. When I was open at those times I was successful in receiving that loving energy that came to them, then through them, to me. They were truly in their divinity. Their examples started to show me a powerful awareness about myself and they were powerful presenters of spiritual and healing information.

Yet there were those who focused so much energy on their humanity. Just as I am writing this, in the moment, I recognize my negative judgment of those who were negatively judging them. So the insight of these souls over the years actually was parallel and related to my insight of my own healing. What was happening to them was happening to me.

### Sunburst

I started to speak at the Sunburst treatment center very early in my recovery. It was one of the first spiritual centers that my then wife was starting to attend, in a church. She had been guided there by a woman, Kathie, who would become a major supporter of my healing, and continues to be now for over twenty years. At the time Kathie was assisting women with reentry into the workforce, and that was how my wife met her and learned of the treatment center.

The center had a support group. I checked it out and began to attend on a regular basis. A large percentage, if not all, of the participants were also involved in a Twelve Step group called "adult children of alcoholics" or A.C.A. It is at this spiritual center that

I was introduced to science and physics which would play a large part in my life path towards healing.

A member of this support group had been speaking as a volunteer at another treatment center. He invited me to ride out with him. We drove out of town, along a narrow, concrete  road with numerous cracks that had been patched over the years. Driving over it made a clackity-clack sound under the tires of the truck. It sounded like a train track. The road was lined by irrigation ditches and, in season, corn grew on both sides of the road. The center had once been used as a place for farm hands to live while working, with small rooms attached to the outside of a large hall. The meetings were held in a large main room flanked by two massive fireplaces.

Huge eucalyptus trees, right next to the buildings, towered over the property and could be seen from quite a distance. Gigantic nests, the size of my truck's hood, nestled in the tops of the trees and served as the homes of many blue herons. These big birds would glide in to roost at dusk, and they looked like prehistoric pterodactyls.

The old complex was run down in many ways, yet it served those who would never have gotten access to services due to the cost of a lot of other treatment centers. So I went to my first meeting and sat next to the guy who had invited me.

He began his talk, and I sat with his audience, listened to him, and wondered if anyone would get anything out of what he was sharing. I had not been out of treatment that long, but it seemed to me that he was mostly interested in impressing them with his intellect, with what he thought he knew. I felt that he was talking at us and not sharing with us. I left with him and didn't know what to say all the way back. Some time later he asked if I would be interested in doing the meeting now that he was done out there. I had not run many meetings in town, so I had some hesitation. Some of that was my lack of ability to read well, and I am sure there were other issues, also. Yet I agreed. It turned out very well for me. What was offered at the spiritual center as it related to science, the leanings toward Native American teachings, and the concept of Emotional Detox, was a great value for me.

The other great component for me was traveling way out there to give my talk and share concepts that were beginning to formulate within me. It was 30 miles from my house. I could speak from my heart, express my process of Emotional Detox and would more than likely never see any of these people ever again. I was sharing from my heart and my heart was very heavy with emotional pain.

It started off as a Twelve Step meeting yet very quickly it transformed into something totally different. For between six to seven years, the last Thursday of the month became a special event that helped me to heal. It was to have an effect on others as well. The center started to open up on Friday mornings to allow a time for processing the energy that was coming out as a result of our gathering the night before. As I look back, I am so grateful to Spirit for setting up a time frame and place for me to expand and share my heart with others. Many of the things I shared there still pertain to me now.

I shared with them that perhaps we are not defective or flawed, but our thoughts, beliefs and perceptions are. Perhaps we were incapable of doing it wrong; perhaps we will alway succeed. We can choose now to have this success in moving into healing or deeper into dis-ease. There is no one to blame and no one at fault; this does not mean we do not take responsibility or accountability for those we hurt, including ourselves.

Yet there is cause and effect. If we understand cause we can change the effect. This is the co-creative power we have within us, to re-create. Because of the energy that was created in the gathering with all of us, I felt confident to make this statement: "I have good news and bad news. The bad news is that we will never successfully use again. The good news is that we will never successfully use again." The power word in these statements is *successfully*.

Wisdom is the cure and wisdom is within us all. The emotional pain we have experienced is not because we have done it wrong. It is because we are doing it right and the pain is evidence of transformation and healing. It is about *Emotional Detox* and *redefining self*, that addiction has little to do with substance, but has more to do with finding anything outside of ourselves to alter our inside perceptions which we have habituated to and then created an identity related to that.

As I write some of the things I shared there, I realize just how much I needed to hear them. Unknown to me, the end was coming for this special place. During that time in which the meeting had transformed, I started the meeting with a song by the Eagles and closed with Diana Ross. I did a ceremony at the very end. Those who wanted to were given the opportunity to make a statement. As they formed a circle, I stood inside and asked each one to say his or her name and follow with *I am*. Not that they were addicts, survivors, codependents or any thing else, but *I am*.

As each soul spoke this out loud, I stood in front of him or her and, if possible, made eye contact. For the few who did not want to be a part of this, I just asked that person to say *pass*. As each shared I would say, "For those of you who want to know how you start this process of transformation, I believe in starting with a statement of truth, and you share that statement of truth with someone who accepts this powerful truth. I believe and accept this truth in this moment about you as I accept it within myself. The process has now begun. It is now up to you to do with it as you choose."

Today there is no evidence that Sunburst existed. The farm that was next to it bought the property and everything was removed. Only a couple of the trees, with the herons still living in them, remain. The ground where the buildings once stood is now part of the farm and covered with a new growth of crops. I wonder about the new growth that came before with those that passed though that place and influenced my own transformation. I tried to calculate how many I shared with in the years that I was there. I figured between 2,500 to 3,000.

I found a very great friend there whose name is Greg. We have supported one another for over eighteen years now. I consider him a true blessing in my life. Please don't tell him I said this.

It may have been the perception that I went to Sunburst to teach, and in some way I did teach some people. But for me the most powerful aspect of that whole experience was what I learned. When Sunburst closed down, I tried other places, but there were other lessons for me to learn not connected to speaking.

In that time shortly after it closed, my father died, which got me reconnected to my family of origin that I had chosen to be detached from for many years. My first grandson was brought into this world—a gift from children. My marriage transformed through a divorce. All that and more were important events for my continued lessons on my journey. I am grateful that I have been blessed to get back into speaking and now writing and life coaching and knowing that as I expand and radiate an energy of healing that others will be affected. Thanks to Spirit, I am less attached to how that affects others. I know my energy has shifted as the law of attraction has brought to me some wonderful souls who support me on my path.

## Love

In all the years I have devoted myself to dying in order to be reborn, many have given me feedback as they watched and supported me on my path. I often did not manage to grasp the depth of what they were sharing.

The first recollection of this was when someone said, "Don't get me wrong"—and I heard it many times—"you sure are hard on yourself." Or "David, why do you beat up on yourself so much?" For what seemed like a long time, those comments really didn't penetrate very deeply within me. Yet another comment did begin shifting my cells. In a men's group, one of the guys radiated the right energy and I guess I was ready to receive the lesson. His statement was simply this: "David, you sure have a lot of self-loathing." Even as I recall this now as I write—and the timespan was many years ago—I can still feel a little of the power that simple statement allowed me to feel at that time. Something about being more open, and the timing in that moment, created a shift within me.

I have been blessed with loving support by those who shared their views on the powerful growth I was expanding toward. They also had the loving courage to help me see myself and the ways I might have been holding back my healing.

There are many terms related to SELF such as self-respect, self-honoring and—the big one for me—self-love. These were only terms to me. I had little to no emotional connection with them.

Many years back when I was speaking to those in the very early stages of their healing, as I was one of them, I shared this statement. "Much of what I am going to share with you is this concept: I am reuniting myself with MY SELF with 'self' being a four letter word to my connection to Spirit." Little did I know I was about to really uncover within me the true power of this statement by asking a pain-filled question. While doing healing work with another teacher, something was coming up and out of me, an energy in motion, hence *emotion*.

This was the question I asked my teacher: "Why is it so hard for me to love myself?" This was her response: "David, loving yourself is not your issue now. Love flows naturally; for right now your healing will expand as you learn to *stop hating yourself*."

That went right to my core. I had been searching for some kind of spiritual solution in my new life, yet at the core of me was little to no respect of self, much loathing of self, and the consistent habitual behavior of beating up on myself. So without awareness, I was in search of my divinity yet hated my humanity. I had little to no awareness that I could not have one without the other. So as I have continued on my path of healing, I have recognized that a giant leap to self-love was too big. As I shared with my support system—which I call my "family of choice"— I had to start with this:

*I will consider it maybe kind of remotely possible to like myself.*

As I have moved forward in that, I know I am moving closer to love. It is showing up in many ways: in the loving souls whom I am attracting, to the ways I feel internally, and how I am having more moments of peace and calm. It was something I had no context for during most of my life: the coming together of my humanity and my divinity to be whole, healed and to be one with spirit and to accept my place in the universe. I wanted to embrace my divinity while hating my humanity. It didn't work..

## How Far Have I Come

Many years later, as an adult, there have been two times that I had to have a gun in my own hands to protect myself and others. In May of 2005 while in my office/studio, which is attached to my home, I was working on my art. I thought I heard a voice outside the open door. I was not sure, but then the sounds of clanging of the iron gates just outside the open door caused me to look outside.

There stood a young traumatized woman. She was naked. I did not immediately understand what she was saying. I heard fragments of sentences that I could pick out: a man, her car, a gun. My first thoughts were that this was some kind of set up, a way of getting into my home with somebody hiding around the corner. Then I looked deep into her eyes and felt the tremendous trauma that she was experiencing. I guided her to the side door, quickly went to my bedroom, and grabbed my gun. I told my partner to call the police and tell them that someone was in trouble outside on the side of the house. I brought a robe to the young woman. My partner helped her and spoke with her and brought her into our home. It was then I placed myself outside my office door and began to pray that no one showed up. I did not know if it was a boyfriend, husband, or stranger who was trying to hurt this tiny lady.

In what seemed like no time at all, dozens of police officers surrounded my house and dispersed throughout the neighborhood, helicopters hovered in the air and police dogs were on the ground, all searching for this perpetrator. Well, my prayer was answered and this guy did not show up.

In those moments before the police got there, I wondered if I could hurt or kill somebody even in the protection of others or myself. I was raised around guns and was trained in safety, but was never trained to be in this situation. I was quickly informed that it was not a boyfriend or a husband; it turned out to be a serial rapist and murderer who had been terrorizing innocent women for a long time. This powerful young woman escaped from him, and, for whatever reason, was guided to my home.

My partner and I went to one of his two trials. Although I never saw the young woman since that time, I was told that she is doing well, considering what she experienced. For myself, I was grateful that no serial rapist had shown up at my home. I was able to share this incident with a few close friends, but there was little emotion connected to the event. This would not be the same experience I would have several years later.

On a September day in 2012 at 5:30 in the morning, I woke up to the loud screams of someone outside my home. As I looked out my front door I saw a man crouched behind my work trailer. He was obviously under the influence and was acting psychotic. I didn't make out too much of what he was trying to say. I went to call the police, and I heard something being thrown around outside. It was then I felt unsafe.

While on the phone with the police, I grabbed my gun. I looked to find where he was in order to inform the police operator. Outside my side door was this guy with a large piece of wood that turned out to be a pick handle he'd taken out of my trailer. He had it positioned over his head as though ready to use it to inflict harm. He was just outside my side door standing behind the hedge next door. He may have been a total of fifteen feet from where I stood, with only the door between us. With my left hand holding the phone to my ear while I talked to the 911 operator and my right hand holding my gun behind my right hip, I began to be very aware of the fragile window panes and the thin wood of the French door between us.

The door was the line in the sand. If he breached the door I would have to act. Then we made eye contact. I'm watching what this guy is going to do next, talking to the operator and my partner is also asking me questions. I became aware of what was going on in my body, emotions, and mind.

In the middle of all this, I started doing something that was very familiar to me. For lack of better description, I fell into feeling very little, feeling incapable of making the right decisions. I felt terror and shame that these are not the feelings of a real man, one who is tough, strong, and decisive. I became aware of this realization and experienced all of this during a few moments while face-to-face with an armed intruder, nothing but this flimsy door between us.

He realized that he'd been seen; he began to very slowly crouch down behind the hedge. I realized I was experiencing not only my own feelings but somehow his energy as well. It seemed to take forever for the police to get there, which in real time was not accurate. They did show up and the guy ran down the street and was picked up, with the pick handle close by him. So it seemed that it was over, yet this was just the beginning of the gift of release of some trauma related to the original story about my father, when I had taken his gun and run from the house.

A short time after the arrest of this guy who had been in my yard, I had the chance to reach out to my friends. The emotions of the event had begun to boil and churn within me. I was very close to a member of my support system who was in the armed services. He had the training to act instinctively. He was very understanding of the feelings that were starting to to be released within me. He told me not to beat myself up and not be so judgmental. To bring some clarity about this, it has been one of my greatest challenges on my path of healing to not be so hard on myself.

He is now a teacher and has been one of many who have been guiding me away from taking and carrying other people's emotional energy. He told me that even as a military policeman, when he had to pull out and discharge his gun, it took him days to get over it and that just this event alone was enough for me to deal with. This helped a little, but I was most helped by his intuitiveness that I was becoming aware of much more that was happening within me. It became clear that this guy came into my life at that moment because I needed him to stimulate stored emotions that were buried deep inside me on a cellular level.

The trauma I felt over the intruder had unleashed, and allowed me to express finally, the emotional trauma that had not been expressed with my dad and the gun, in that incident from my childhood when I had run from the house with the gun only to discover it wasn't loaded. When I had looked at that guy, face-to-face, eyeball-to-eyeball, I was looking at my father's face. Both were equally psychotic; both were equally out of control. How could I ever imagine these two incidents would be linked and allow me to expand into a level of Emotional Detox that would be part of my journey towards self love?

It astounds me that it took 48 to 49 years, the time between these events, to be open and ready to release and let go in order to be free. This, plus other similar events that I had been experiencing in the months previous that were just as powerful, allowed me to feel a calmness in mind and my body. I also felt a level of compassion toward my father that I had resisted most of my life. I had felt compassion toward the intruder because when I looked in his eyes, I finally saw my father's eyes. I guess steps toward forgiveness aren't always warm and fuzzy. I am more aware and amazed by where and how teachers show up. I am equally amazed by the power of Emotional Detox, however long it takes.

### Adult - Child

It took me some time to really grasp the power of the term *adult child*. I have always had major emotional issues related to the whole inner child concept from when I first heard about it. The only relationship I had with it was to say, "I have been forty-five years old most of my young life." I felt serious and angry and, most of all, filled with terror, even though others may have seen me in a different light. When I first heard the term *precious inner child*, I was repulsed by it. I was unable to accept that. Most of my life I had been very emotionally immature, and I did not have any kind of precious feeling about it at all. The other concept that eluded me was that I was born perfect and somehow knowing I was connected to god.

I really believe the shift in me started when I watched a television program on one of the science channels. It showed in detail the complete process of conception. I had watched many programs related to this, starting in third grade when we had a special meeting separate from the girls. Over the years, I was introduced to many programs, but this was the most detailed and was done with the latest technology to show the entire process.

I was totally amazed by how much goes on throughout that process of creation. The journey of the male cells and all that they encounter: that alone is a story all of its own. What is odd to me is that when I have shared in detail that intriguing process with groups, it has been the guys who seem to have the most discomfort. I guess *macho* only goes so far. I was struck by the incredible complexity of how those cells interacted with one another during their search for the female egg and the technology of actually having cameras placed within the body to show the true process. I realized what I had been exposed to previously wasn't accurate. I had been shown a film that showed numerous male cells surrounding the female egg, but that film had been made in a laboratory setting and outside the body in a petrie dish. I began to see that a multitude of male cells surrounding the female egg was a simplification. The truth was that a few, more likely just one, male cell succeeds in this incredible journey to unite.

For the first time I began to see that just to have been conceived, to be here, is a miracle. With all the religious, inspirational talks, the motivational books and audio that I had been involved with for years, it was this program that helped me see the miracles we are.

So this should be it. I got it. I'm done. It was the greatest lesson learned—well, maybe not. Because my next awareness was to ask, "What the hell happened?" I didn't feel like a miracle, even with all this awareness. Then I was introduced to Bruce Lipton's book, *The Biology of Belief.*

I aways felt that I had been affected by negativity while inside my mother. What The *Biology of Belief* did for me was to remove the morality judgment that somehow I was wrong or bad. It allowed me to understand I was an absorber of energy way before I was birthed from my mother. The entire environment both inside and out was affecting my mother and so how could it not have affected me? I would love to talk to Oprah Winfrey and explain that sometimes "aha moments" are not warm and fuzzy. Sometimes they are more like "*aahh, shit"!*

I gained a sense of validation from reading Bruce Lipton's book. It became clear to me, given many factors, why I did not recall most of my early childhood. There seemed to be this perfect combination of factors that created my emotional future. I learned that when someone begins to drink and use, emotional growth is slowed.

I believe my emotional growth was slowed even before I began to drink and use. I had entered the world with a perfect combination of factors. My own internal experiences; the external trauma going on with my mother; the environment and actions between the entire family related to our parents' behaviors; my placement in the family; my own hyperemotional sensitivity. All of this set up a life filled with immature emotions, which got stuck in a growing physical body.

The perfect mix, to put it in the context the adult-child model, was what "made" me. It's no wonder I searched for someone who would give me the right answers, guide me, so I would not have to feel so lost and defective. Given all this, I have done well in the adult word. The downside for me is that it has rarely felt okay emotionally. It did not take much stimulus for me to internally react in complete panic, which to look grown up would usually come out as anger. Most of my life was wanting to find something or someone who would make me feel safe and adult or maybe, to use a better term, *mature*. In the beginning of my journey of healing, I was very disappointed and it scared the hell out of me to realize that the person I was searching for was *me*. So much of my recovery life has been learning how to grow up.

I liken much of it to a vision quest: searching to understand the identity I had created in order to survive emotionally, and letting go of the wounded parts of me that no longer served my healing. It has been, and still is at times, a challenge to release the past that I had been so attached to.

I am a big guy and my facial construct may come across as somewhat menacing. I come across as looking serious or even angry. It was a look that was described to me by my sister-in-law when she first met me when I was a child. So as confusing as it might be for others, it has been doubly so for me.

I am grateful to those that have looked deeper and have seen me in a different light. I have alway felt distant from most children, the reason being obvious to me now. So when I heard from those who stated that part of their mission was to help children, it took me some time to realize that I want to help children, too. They just happen to be in grown-up bodies, those like myself who were adult children.

## Punishment and profit

It strikes me as strange when two separate experiences can come together somehow to make some weird connection. So this story will now jump from childhood punishment to remodeling swimming pool decking. Okay, let me see if I can explain this so it will make some sense. A friend offered me the opportunity to give a training at a health care agency. He stated that I could promote my desire to do more training and also promote my contracting business if I could find a way to tie the two together. My response was, "I know how without any problem."

First I have to go back to my early childhood and recall how my mother punished us by making us kneel on the bathroom floor.

Some years later I am a young man, fresh out of high school and have no idea or plan for my future. To be quite honest, I was scared to hell and totally emotionally unprepared for my life.

My father had his own company in the swimming pool decking construction business. The last couple of years of school I worked for him during summer vacation, so it was easy to just go into working in his company once I graduated. His company did what is known as new construction.We poured the concrete around newly constructed pools. After some time with his company I started to take over his warranty repairs. This meant I would go out and patch and repair decks. This allowed me to meet and talk directly to the home owners. I liked it and enjoyed explaining what I was going to do as it related to the repairs. I can see now how this was preparing me for my future of starting my own business and would also facilitate my speaking and now my writing.

About the time I started with my father's company, a new style of pool deck was being introduced to the industry. It was called a cantilever interior. This meant that the pool deck extended slightly into the pool about two inches and below that was the water line tile. Sometimes the bottom edges of this cantilever would break off.

My father could out-work any five guys, yet he did not have a lot of skill in detail. He loved epoxy and used gray tape on everything. After watching him do a repair I remember thinking it looked terrible. At some point, I stated doing his repair work.

I started to realize that there was another factor that needed to be addressed in order to truly have the repair last. So many years later on my path to healing, this is the lesson learned from these repairs: if you do not address the cause, you can never change the effect.

Another important insight to this topic called *punishment and profit* was this: it's about remembering how we were punished and relating this to the unique repair work on the cantilever edge of the pool deck.

See, I would have to be on my knees, leaning over into the the pool with my head just above the water in order to do this type of repair. All the pressure was on my knees and lower back. I punished myself in the same manner my mother had punished me. For many years doing this work, I rarely used any protection for my knees. It now seems incredible to me how I continued my own abuse. I still take a lot of pride in the work I have done in my business, yet I am growing with more self-love in the work. As I continue with my transformation, I do not want to punish myself any more.

## Focus: Where I Have to Go and What I Have to Accomplish

When I started doing my own work in the construction business and the pool-deck industry, I had more or less been fired from my own father's company. At the time it was traumatic. I received minimal support from my father, though I was able to do jobs through his company as a service. I had bought one of the old work trucks that was used up and too small for my father's growing business. The truck was a lot like me. It was beat to hell and just would not quit running. Trust me, there were times I tried to kill it.

Oddly enough, as I reflect back and compare the truck and myself, I understand it was not much of a stretch to see how close I came to killing myself, sometimes in the truck. I named it Barabbas after the prisoner released in the place of Jesus. I remember the movie: he was destined to live a troubled life and couldn't die.

So this beater truck and I started finding jobs, all related to repair work, whereas my father's company was based in new construction. By selling my own work, I would sell directly with homeowners. I did not have to deal with any large company employees, like sales personnel and supervisors, which I found difficult to do (something related to issues with authority figures—or another possibility: authority figures having issues with me).

I started with minimal equipment, so a lot of my work was somewhat primitive. Instead of using electric power tools, I did most of my early work by hand. I did not have the finances to invest in good tools when I first started working for myself.

I used a hammer and chisel to widen large cracks in preparation for repairs. Then I would resurface with new cool deck to cover the repair.

I was hired to repair a semi-public pool at an apartment complex. The crack was about two feet from the water's edge and went all the way around the large pool. I picked my starting point and started preparing the crack by opening it up with a hammer and chisel. I worked in the direction of the crack, facing toward the work I had to do. As I kneeled, I looked up constantly. I could have sworn that crack was bending over the horizon of the earth's curve.

As I consistently looked up, I noticed the crack growing longer. I noticed that it went *all the way around the whole pool*. I had just started and was already thinking I should have charged more.

I made a decision. Instead of facing the direction of where I needed to go, I turned around so I could only see the progress I was making. Only once in a while, when I turned to see how much was left, would I get overwhelmed. At some point I realized I was making progress, and I finished that phase of the preparation. This experience occurred many years before I started the major shift toward healing.

I've looked back to that experience at times and wondered if the message was there for me to get ready for the journey.

Many times throughout this process I focused on how far I had to go, not looking at or honoring how far I have progressed. Many times I am hard on myself and in judgment that my focus is not right. Thanks to the great and blessed support of souls who remind me of my dedication, I am able to look at the powerful changes I have made. I know it is happening within me.

## Trying to Not Be an A-hole

I seem to have a bit of a reputation for sometimes being blunt. I know that over the years, I have attracted a support system of souls who have helped me to "soften" my linguistic abilities. So after years of association with these people, I hear myself saying things differently. I don't believe that my intent in the past was to be mean, but I know I carried a lot of anger. It may not have been only what I said, but also the energy with which I stated it. I don't apologize at all for my feedback to most with whom I shared. With many of those with whom I was interacting, I somehow sensed it was appropriate for me to share in this manner. Others, of course, were taken aback. Then after getting to know me and that my intent was truly to be honest and supportive of them, they were more at ease.

I feel many were able to know that I meant well, although some did not manage to do this. My response to this would have been something like, "I don't care about how they feel about how I state my opinion." I didn't realize that the term *don't care* had, to some, a negative connotation. The reality is the true definition of the word *care* makes my statement somewhat accurate even though I was not aware of it until recently.

So when my timing is right—and I can remember—my response might be like this, "I am not attached to how others respond." I still feel odd even to write it, let alone to say it. At least I am working on it.

My comments that contain an angry energy usually come in response to hearing someone making a statement that I feel is self-deprecating. This is something I am still very sensitive to, having been this way for so much of my own life. It's something I consistently watch for with myself even now. I have attracted a group who supports me and confronts me when I slip up once and awhile.

At this point in my life I am grateful for the growth of self-acceptance I have made related to this issue. Much of what I have become aware of about myself is, for lack of better description, that I am *grounded* or *earthy*. I am accepting of my own outside-the-box ways of seeing how the world works or, more importantly, how we work within the world. That, for me, speaks of how we are all energy, of how we are created from the stars. Sometimes, perhaps sounding like some hippie freak, my response is to say *cool*. It still strikes me as strange that I react to others who I sense are using these ideas as an intellectual way of being dissociated from themselves and their emotions.

This is an example of what I mean. I was part of a men's group that is affiliated with a spiritual teaching center. It was based in the teachings of Ernest Holmes and the Science of Mind. I started being involved with it shortly after the 9/11 tragedy in New York. I had some impact on the group, I believe, with my overt emotions and my willingness to express my discomfort with walking my path to healing, which I would define as *Emotional Detox*. We were going to have a retreat in Sedona. I was looking forward to my first time participating in a structured event like this.

There were lots of private introspective exercises. One of them required that we not speak to one another and just study ourselves from within as we walk into the wilderness. I walked along Oak Creek and found a spot to sit on a large boulder. I had brought with me one of my own personal medicine rattles that I had made. The rattle was made from a gourd with a mesquite branch handle, adorned with leather, beads, small bells and special feathers.

While sitting watching the water, listening and working at quieting my mind, I started looking at this rattle in more detail, and although I love the grain of mesquite—especially on this one particular rattle—I gazed into the water, watching the motion as it flowed around the rocks, then at the same time gazed back at the rattle. I then realized that the motion of the water was captured in the grain of the rattle's handle. The grain moved around the knots just as the water flowed around the rocks. The medicine of the water was always in the rattle. I may have never made that connection had it not been for this experience.

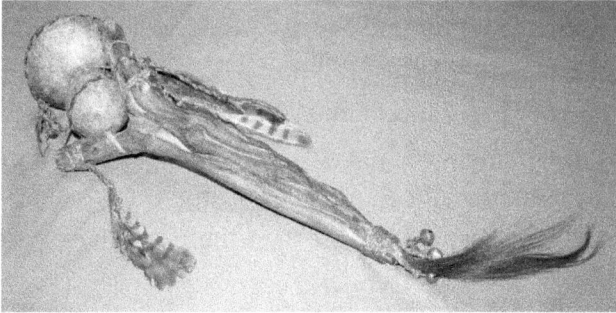

David's personal medicine rattle, artwork he designed and created, which he took with him on the retreat in Sedona

Another exercise was done as a group. We gathered together, created a circle, and sat outside in the cool clean air. The mild breeze was comforting. The facilitator talked to us for a while about having a male figure in our lives that we may or may not have shared with in our pasts.

He asked, "If you had the chance to talk to any male figure, who would it be?" The guy to my left said he would like to talk with Ernest Homes, the center of the thought process of Science of Mind. The man next to him said he wanted to speak to Buddha. As each guy mentioned more men like Jesus or Einstein, I felt detached and confused and actually annoyed. So I was last to share. I stayed quiet for a moment.

Inside my mind I was wondering if I was not connected to wanting to know at a higher level because I had no desire to communicate with any of these men. All this happened in a tiny fraction of a second, and I again had the old thought from my grade school days that I was less intelligent than those around me. Then, this was my response:

"I have no desire to meet or talk to any of these men. Maybe there is something wrong with me. Perhaps it is my low self-esteem, I don't know. The only men I would like to confront are my abusive alcoholic grandfather and father."

My voice began to crack with emotion. "I would love to ask them both what the f--k happened that we created this in our family?"

After a moment of silence the participants of this exercise began to share from their hearts rather from their intellects. The energy completely transformed as the depth of sharing got deeper. It was not my intent to alter the group and my only intent was to expand my own healing. I am not attached to how that affects others. All I do is accept that as I stay on my path and continue the journey into self-love, I will resonate with a radiant energy that will continue to expand around me and it will affect others.

**Emotional Detox** is accepting that thoughts, perceptions and beliefs are creative energies that can be healing or can create dis-ease. The energy of our mind is stored in every cell of our bodies, and we constantly replace those cells with new cells. We infuse the new cells with the same old energy, thus reinforcing the old perception and beliefs and our dis-ease. Or we can choose to infuse the new cells with new thoughts, perceptions, and beliefs, and we can then overcome or replace the dis-ease and move into a deeper level of healing.

# TEACHERS

## It Amazes Me

I am consistently sharing my gratitude to those souls who surround me. These are souls who support me on my path toward expanded healing. I made the decision to redefine my life, and I have attracted many who have offered me their respect and love. What amazes me is the diversity of all those around me. How different our backgrounds and thoughts, yet our paths have crossed.

I met some very special people at a very pivotal time in my life. One of these persons is a teacher of the healing power of vibration and harmonics, Dr. Harold

Moses. I was introduced to him and the people whom he attracted to his teachings. He had been educated in music and is a concert violinist. I, on the other hand, had no experience in singing or music, yet I was attracted to the energy that radiated when I was present with him. I met him at the time that my relationship with my then wife was shifting and our 30-year marriage was coming to and end.

Harold and his wife Laura were very giving of their support, as were many within the group they had attracted. Harold and I became good friends; he was not one who shared a lot about his path. I, on the other hand, can reflect back and recognize that I was very stuck to my story, especially when it came to talking about the overt feelings I was experiencing and how I wanted to understand what I was thinking. It took me a while to begin to see my pattern. I would share these profound emotions with him, and he would respond with, "It is only vibration." It was confusing at best and would piss me off. Only years later did I begin to see the connection to how he was responding. He was not completing the cycle of my emotional story; my anger came from thinking he did not understand, so inside myself I judged him. I assumed he must have been detached from his own feelings.

What I have come to understand is that he was allowing me to do what I was going to do, and he had no need to take it on himself or be part of the expansion of my discomfort by talking about it with me . . . or he just didn't care. Actually, we had great talks together and I considered him one of my many great teachers. I did not know much of his history—I'm sure I told him of mine although perhaps not in detail. One of my habits was to tell all. The reason I mention this is to express my amazement at how we attracted one another.

Harold was going to do a talk about the path of healing work he is involved with. I had heard him speak many times before, yet this time he mentioned something I never knew about him as it related to his mother. It moved me emotionally, deeply. He shared that when he was still inside his mother, she sat at the piano and played classical music to him.

His following message about the healing powers of vibration as it related to singing and music was totally lost by me. All I could think about was that statement about his mother's interaction with him as a fetus. All I could do was try to understand what was coming up for me emotionally. It was some time later in his talk that it came to me what was stirring inside. As I heard talk about his mother, I started reflecting back to my own experience while I was inside my mother. From all indications, classical music was not what I was experiencing.

My experience as a fetus was the trauma and drama of what my mother was going through. All indications, from what I know of her life at that time, is that she had all she could deal with just to survive the toxic relationship she and my father had created together. This was not what amazed me, though. It was that Harold and I came from such powerfully contradictory upbringings, at least in the very beginnings of our development, and yet we were there together on this spiritual journey. It was realizing how supportive to one another we were as we walked this path, knowing that we probably would have had nothing to do with one another had we met in the past.

It's strange at times to have this elevated energy of others supporting me. At times it has been very uncomfortable due to my carried-over feeling of being undeserving of this degree of support. The level of communication is a blessing to me. Even though it can still be light and silly, the basis of our conversations, with this core of my family of choice, is about the expansion of knowing. We support one another in our transformation towards a new knowing. I have even created a healing circle with regular meetings as well as what is called a greatness circle.

On of my powerful teachers hosts a supper club. In this process she creates a wonderful dinner and attracts like-minded souls to come together. The conversation is always in a beautiful, loving, supportive direction of healing. Kathie was one of my first spiritual mentors from over twenty years ago. We lost connection for a while, then reconnected several years ago. In that reconnection, she told me she was teaching classes at a halfway house and invited me to go and share my talk with one of her classes. We taught together for the next two and a half years, until they closed down the classes due to money issues. We have been close ever since. She is, again, another blessing in my life.

When I first met Kathie, I was in the deepest of my Emotional Detox, much of it related to my family of origin and the family I was co-creating with my wife at that time. In one of our meetings, Kathie handed me a book, *Illusions* by Richard Bach. I opened it to a page somewhere in the middle of the book. I now use the quotation that appeared on that page to close many of my talks: "The bond that links your true family is not one of blood, but of respect and joy in each other's life. Rarely do members of one family ever grow up under the same roof."

Another quote from *Illusions* is, "Here is a test to know if your mission on Earth is complete. If you are still here, it isn't."

I feel blessed with the souls whom I have attracted on my way towards rediscovering myself and for my role in the support of others. In sharing with others, I have plowed through heavy emotional discomfort as well as the calm of being in the moment. I have experienced a little judgment that was only the reflection of where they perceived me on my path, and I now receive total support in love. Yes, it is interesting that I have attracted into my life this incredible group of souls. I never want to devalue anybody's path that he or she has chosen, especially in regards to education and how that is related to those in health care who are offering support to so many who need help. The effort, time, and money needed to complete that education should be honored and respected. I feel that I do so to all those who have worked so hard to have paper.

I have met great teachers, trainers and therapists with all kinds of letters in front of and behind their names. I have been blessed with some who have participated in a healing circle that I also am a part of. It has been my honor to watch those who went deep within themselves and began their own healing process. I watched them become even greater in their skills to help others because their energy expanded within them and thus radiates from them. This aids their clients just by walking in the door.

They have transformed into healers by bringing healing energy that surrounds those they are in contact with. I feel very honored that in my own healing I have been able to be of support to them even though my education comes from a practical environment. I, like many others, have come through massive trauma and have fought back to reclaim the power and wisdom we gave away as children in order to survive.

Do not discount the work and efforts that we have come through to heal ourselves, of course with the support of others. We can and will radiate that energy of healing that can affect others, even without paper. I can admit that there may be thoughts that do discount, yet the challenge for me and others is letting go of discounting ourselves. It is something I am working through as evidenced by writing this now. I have forged forward on my own hero's journey as described by Joseph Campbell.

One of my many teachers introduced to me the term *clairsentience*. I had never heard of this word before. I started to research its meaning and found one definition: feeling or sensation as distinguished from perception and thought beyond the range of normal perception. Normal perception? This allowed me to have a better understanding of things I had stated for years, like how I realized that I believed I was caring for others, but the reality was I was carrying others.

This was yet another example of saying that I felt bad for my father, and how I have done this with so many others throughout my life.

It has been really important for me to understand that I was not broken, flawed or defective. When I heard terms such as clairvoyance (seeing beyond the range of ordinary perception) or clairaudience (the power or faculty of hearing something not present to the ear but regarded as having objective reality), I began to recognize that some people have these qualities early in their lives. They might have been afraid to own them at first, or to share with others. Some may have believed they were somehow mentally ill or crazy, only later to find they were not. Then they might try to help others understand a gift that could help themselves and others.

I now see how easy it was for me to have no ability to understand this thing called *clairscentience*. It's no wonder I thought I was emotionally and mentally ill most of my life. I began to learn how to deal with what I had believed to be a disorder, and started to believe it was an extended, expanded tool for my own healing.

Yet the attraction to others, again in the beginning, would model that which I was familiar with. I could start to see that many that I chose to get close to were just extensions of those I had attracted from my family of origin and others who represented that throughout my life. Yet, little by little, I embraced change in my behaviors and, more importantly, the redefining of beliefs and perceptions. The energy that I resonated with changed, thus beginning a shift in those I was attracted to and those who have been attracted to my new transforming self.

## Children

A recent Father's Day allowed a deeper understanding for myself related to the men, or at least male figures, in my life. I have shared my times through these writings about my divorce after thirty years.

At the time of the divorce, over ten years ago now, my daughter and two sons were young adults. As my ex-wife divorced me, so too did my sons. My daughter and I have kept in constant contact throughout and are very close. She is a powerful healer in my life.

In regards to my sons, we have had little to no contact at all. I have wanted to accept this as an understanding of their hurt and anger and, more than likely, disappointment that they have in me as well as for the lifetime of dysfunction that the marriage put them through.

They have chosen to not be involved with me. I respect this and look at it as an opportunity to focus on my own healing. For me to move on and basically grow up, grow into my maturity, I had to accept that they are adults now and have their own paths to walk, their own lessons to learn.

My intention, my focus on what I need to do in order to move beyond the past, will help me deal differently with my sons should they choose to reconnect. As a healthier person, I would not have to blame anybody or spend energy defending myself, or the big one: not have to feel the need to council them or advise them. If they choose not to reconnect with me, I will have still benefited by doing my own work on myself.

Much of the separation with my sons had little emotional context for me at the time.

It was the gifting from my daughter of a hand-crafted Father's Day present that brought the buried emotions of the past up from within me. At the same time that I felt honored by this heartfelt gift from my daughter, it allowed me to release the hurt and disappointment over the relationships with my sons.

This experience also brought up for me all my past male relationships, from family members to those associates I called friends at the time. Whether with intent or not, I alway felt somewhat disrespected, misunderstood, and isolated. I coped by doing everything I could to gain respect and to be understood. In doing so, I gave myself away in order to try to fit in. I did this even if fitting in was uncomfortable and many times demeaning. I had a desperate need to defend or explain myself.

This gift from my daughter, given from her loving, pure heart on a holiday which brought me great discomfort— as do most, if not all, holidays—allowed me to release energy that had been stored in every cell of my body. The gifts and lessons I have gained from my daughter, from the true love she radiates from her soul, still amaze me. For those of us who have labeled her as special needs, I realize that those who are considered average, normal or healthy may be in special need to be accepting of the unconditional love from someone like my daughter, who is a healer with nothing more than the energy that resonates from her being.

What really moved me was that the relationship I had created with my sons was so much like the relationships I was raised and surrounded with. I went on, as an adult, to attract fellowship with many who helped me recreate the same dynamics. Then with small shifts within myself, I started attracting new relationships, and those would shift and expand as I was shifting and expanding within myself.

As I reflect upon how far I have come in my all my relationships, especially with men, I realize I have expanded my healing in that area. I now attract others with whom I no longer have to put myself down before anyone else does. I don't have to feel and act defensive or even offensive with others. I'm free to share a point of view without being ridiculed or slashed with sarcasm. Now the people I am surrounded with respect and honor me, and I am capable of doing the same back. We are in support of one another. I honor all my past relationships and respect them all as having been powerful teachers for me in one way or another.

### Delayed Acceptance

Many years ago, not too long after we were married and moved into our home, I got into my truck to run an errand. As I turned the corner driving north I saw an elderly lady struggling to pull a cart on wheels. She was at the edge of a lot that had been vacant for many years. While in high school we used it as a shortcut to the pool hall that was located down the road.

The lot was elevated and had worn down little hills over most all of the surface. Yet through the years small paths were created by those who cut across it. As I drove closer, I saw that she struggled to push her cart on wheels up a small incline. Then she tried pulling it, with equal effort. I drove past her, then looked back through the rear view mirror. I stopped, backed up, and got out of the truck. Concerned that I might scare her, I asked if I could help in some way. She said that if she didn't get her cart up on the first run it was some effort to get it up to the more level ground. I asked where she was going and she said she was going to the grocery store on the corner. It was not a long distance for her yet she had expended a lot of energy to get the cart up the incline.

I said, "If you are okay with it, I can put your cart in the back of the truck and drive you over there." She agreed, so I assisted her in putting the cart in the back of the truck.

As I opened the door to get in she began to ramble. I was only able to get bits and pieces of was she was saying. With little to no gaps between her sentences, she went on and on. She said she was from Texas and that the people in Texas were so much better than those in Arizona. This started to piss me off, due to the fact I am a native of Arizona. She went on and on and, from the fragments of what I could get, she said that the men in Texas were so much better; the people of Texas were so much better. It was not more than a couple of minutes, the longest delay was getting a gap in traffic to make a right turn, so in that short time I wondered how I volunteered for this. I got out of the truck, opened the door for her, and unloaded her cart. She was still talking as I walked back into the truck. I heard her say, "Thank you. I think I just met a Texan."

I didn't clearly absorb what she said because I just wanted to get away. It was a long time after—and I mean a long time after—before I realized she had given me her ultimate compliment. This little old lady whom I encountered for not more than ten to fifteen minutes was sent to me by spirit to be an angel and allow me the opportunity to understand that teachers are everywhere and to be open to lessons wherever and whenever they are offered. Was this something that I got in the moment? No, but I am grateful, no matter whatever length of time it had taken, that I did get it. I do not have to be so reactive to the manner in which lessons are offered to me. The big one for me is to not be so hard on myself and beat myself up over not getting IT sooner, even when I am not sure what IT is.

Was this a pattern of being resistant due to my overt reaction to how others deliver their lessons? The key is being aware of my reaction to whomever is delivering the lesson. Something that has been so easy to witness in others, is now something for me to look at within myself. I am starting to be aware of my habit of instantly reacting with resistance and defensiveness when given a different perspective.

I will be realistic and accept that my first reaction may be very familiar, yet my goal is to place energy on an alternate reaction. It is of great value to be centered and in a place of calm and peace. Perhaps the time of my acceptance will not be so delayed in the future. Perhaps next time I won't have a need to judge the teacher.

# NOW

So after thirty years of marriage and with our children grown to adulthood, my wife and I divorced and everybody moved out, and the energy began to shift. My life transformation started in 1986 when I owned up to addiction and started to change the way I was thinking, believing, and behaving. After the divorce, this process within me accelerated as did the energy of the house, especially after I started a men's group with another friend whom I had met at a spiritual center. I wanted to have the group at my home, and we did. This group transformed to a healing circle.

The new circle gave me the opportunity to share my perspective of the energy of this home. I shared the combined 55-plus years of alcoholic dysfunction and trauma that flowed through this house with the previous owners and then continued by myself and my wife.

Yet now it is a home of healing. People who walk in for the first time state that they feel the healing energy. Some sit in silence through the group and take in what they need: healing energy. Even though I still struggle, there is a part of me that knows others are feeling the transformation that I have done within me and in this home.

It amazes me to look back at what I had attracted from my past as it was falling away, and new souls were there to support me in the pain and discomfort of my own transition. Still living in the same house, I reached out to Susan with whatever support I could offer her from what I had learned in my own journey of healing. We were not very close in thoughts during the years she lived next door with my friend Troy. As a matter of fact, in that time when I was still drinking, I had been very inappropriate with her. Thank god she accepted my offer to make amends to her many years before.

The other amazing aspect of all this is that there are a few who came from that past and now play a role in my new present. Susan has been a powerful teacher for me on this journey I am dedicated to walking.

## Perception-Deception-Side Effects

I will admit that because of where I started on this journey, I have certain biases. Much of this has to do with advertisements that I allow myself to react to. I also accept the understanding of the law of attraction and what I was familiar with from my past.

Let me try to clarify: I have a strong reaction to alcohol advertisements, from one extreme to the other. On the one side is the image of the sophisticated, well dressed, highly imaged, successful, upper management group. As I will accept that this image might be realized somewhere, I was not attracting these people into my realm of drinking and using buddies, so there might be some jealousy involved with this image for me, or not.

Many years ago I was with a good friend at an upper class restaurant on Central Avenue in Phoenix. We ordered our meals right at the time that many of the offices were closing up. So we saw a slow trickle of well-suited white-collared business types, at least this was my perception. As these guys walked in about the time we were being served our salads, I glanced one or two times at these guys who were gathering at the bar. To me they looked just like the marketing I saw advertised. As my friend and I continued on to the completion of our salads, there was a notable increase in the volume of the group at the bar that began to include some very stylish women. As we were served our main dish of steak, potatoes and vegetables, all beautifully arranged, we started to enjoy our meal. From the bar the energy was increasing. I noticed the sarcasm going louder, covered up with even louder laughter: you can't have one without the other. At least that was my experience.

As we finished our dinner and our desserts arrived, we were enjoying our conversation related to the changes we were dedicated to in our healing. I noticed as we talked that we had to increase our volume to compensate for the volume from the bar. By the time it took us to have a nice long dinner, the transformation of the group went from this beautiful sophisticated image to grabbing ass and insulting one another.

Some of the women had coupled up with some of the guys and were making out like they were in a sleazy motel. So, take away all the fancy environment, clothing and image. I was watching the bunch of us from the blue collar world of my past. I was somewhat amazed by the transformation that occurred in such a short time.

This leads me into the realm of advertising to the blue collar world as it related to beer. Back in the day, one beer was considered the "champagne of bottled beer." The same crowd that was shown in these ads was at the upscale restaurant bar we were in. I was drawn to that image and that became my beer of choice for awhile. Then I guess price and volume became an issue so getting more for less became a priority. What amazes me is how the marketing has changed. From the champagne of bottled beer to attract a more sophisticated clientele to what that same beer is marketed towards today.

So I have asked myself, "If it's true that the marketing is not geared towards children, then what is the mental construct behind what is directed to the adults? What is it that their research has told them would be their demographic?" The dumbing down of our society has played itself out well in this marketplace.

This brings up another aspect of this whole thing called marketing. While watching a Wayne Dyer program, I noticed him mentioning how programs that we are saturated with are all about trauma and drama and the news that is consistently putting out fear, anger and resentment towards others. This plays a part in creating dis-ease in our culture. He then said that after that is a commercial to sell you medications that will help you deal with this dis-ease, but will have numerous side effects.

I can now see an extension from that: another ad will follow and offer a drug that will help you deal with the side effects created by the original meds, and then adds a list of more side effects; but let's not stop there. On another advertisement, we see how some lawyers will place a lawsuit against the pharmaceutical industry that has caused us more dis-ease by taking the medication that was supposed to help with the original dis-ease, which may have been caused by the influx of negative information that might have tapped into something triggered from our past that was never resolved.

I am not saying that the use of medications is not useful in aiding in the healing process as long as it at least is given to someone with the hope that his or her own power of self healing is paramount. Here's a case in point: I was watching a commercial when a claim was made by the makers of a medical product—I think it was related to ending smoking tobacco. It is hard sometimes to determine what some of these commercials are even supposed to be helping with. Anyway, I heard this claim that there was a 40 % success rate over the 18% who had taken a placebo. Then came a list of all the possible side effects.

The first thing I thought was what defines success? Then in that same instant, I wondered, "Why in the hell aren't we focusing on the percentage of those who created success with their minds, and what were their side effects from that? And if there are side effects, what other ways can we empower those to use new thoughts, beliefs, and perceptions followed by new behaviors to deal with those side effects?" I am not against the pharmaceutical industry. What I am for is empowerment to allow us to play a larger role in our own healing. Perhaps that can start by redefining ourselves and understanding the power of Emotional Detox.

Many things are now happening in my life including my own transformation that I am dedicated to, and the challenges I seem to put on that process. There are other factors affecting my life. The current shift in the world economy is allowing me to look deeper within myself. I am doing what I can to keep my home and hold on to my business. At the same time, I am faced with some important lessons of letting go. I would love it to be all warm and fuzzy, yet right now it is not. I understand that much of what I am feeling may be related to my history, and that my feelings are shifting. I pray for a rich and loving outcome and work toward accepting it may not look the way I would like it to look.

## *Cloud Atlas* in This Life

The movie and book *Cloud Atlas* raised the notion of us coming back over and over in different lifetimes. In writing about this, it is amazing to me that the same souls in this lifetime can and do affect us. In the transformation of my friend Troy and the shift in my relationship with my ex-wife, I have gained tremendous, yet at times a very painful, healing and a coming together of those I could never have imagined. In wanting to help Troy's longtime partner of over twenty years, I gained a better understanding of myself and of those I had attracted in my past.

Susan has become one of my most powerful teachers as both my ex-wife and Troy had been in my journey inward toward MY SELF. At the time of this writing, we have been together more than eight years. Perhaps only Spirit knows the outcome of lessons to be learned from this relationship, as I stay dedicated to my path of healing.

Sue has told about an awareness that she had as a young girl. She was in the car with her parents while visiting with her grandparents. This was years before she ever met Troy. At the time, her grandparents lived just down the street from what would be Troy's house and my house. Susan recalled that as a young girl she looked up the street toward our homes and had some sort of reaction to looking directly at the houses. She could describe in detail the vehicles parked in the driveway. She would, within the next ten years, be living in one of those houses for over twenty years, and at the time of this writing now lives in the house next door.

So you never know who will or won't be there as you expand on a healing path. Harold Moses was there to teach me songs that enabled me to release those that were moving on a different journey than mine. I have attracted others, even some from my past, and we are now of support to one another in the present moment.

I have another close supporter. His name is Greg. I met him some 18 years ago. He is a very special soul in my life. He was the only one I spoke to about the dysfunction in my marriage and the challenges and frustrations of trying to be a parent. He speaks his mind to me, and when I told him about the divorce, this is how he responded: "Now you and your soon-to-be ex will not have each other to deflect what you need to heal within yourselves as individuals." Not too long ago I was telling him about having this incredible group of souls who support me. He picked up on my emotional tone and said that the way I was stating this sounded like I felt undeserving of these people's support.

This statement allowed me to recognize that I had attracted this supportive group by the shifting of energy that radiates from within me. The diversity of each individual within this group still amazes me. I am blessed with so many more of these special persons than the ones I have mentioned in this writing, some for just a moment, others for many years. To all of you I send love, light and healing energy.

## Self-Judgment

I was sharing with one of my teachers about something that had come up for me, related to my emotions and thoughts and my judgments of them. I shared with Kathie who was my very first spiritual mentor.

"I am more aware of the powerful, overt, toxic and negative self-judgment that I have towards myself."

Kathie has been there for me for many years, as far back as when I first started on this path over twenty-six years ago, and has supported me on my journey. This was her simple statement back to me, "Wow, that was descriptive."

Something inside me was activated. I could not really put my finger on it at that time, yet sharing this comment a few days later with my Zen buddy Greg—we have known each other for over eighteen years—helped a lot. He said, "It has nothing to do with negative judgment, no matter how descriptive you want to be in defining it. It is just about judgment." Between the two of them, I began assessing that for myself. It is just about my judgment.

I had habituated a way of thought based on being very hard on myself. Ask anyone who has walked side-by-side with me over the years that I have been on this healing path. I am sure that the two souls I just mentioned would testify to that. My emotions my whole life have been huge, to the point that it has been an equally huge focus of my teaching. In the beginning, whenever I perceived my emotions as overwhelming or painful, my natural instinct, or—more accurately—my perception, was that it was caused by me being bad or doing something bad or wrong. On the other side of that, the few times I had momentary feelings of joy or happiness, it was generally short-lived and many times came from a place of some sort of sarcastic remark. I suspect that those feelings of contentment only came when I was focused on something outside of myself.

When anyone suggested that I was being hard on myself or self-loathing, I could feel the resistance inside my body, so much so that I really had little concept of what they were sharing with me. If not out loud, at least in my head, I could hear the "yeah, buts." I can see now, looking back, that I identified so strongly with this belief, this perception I had created for myself, that I could not sense anything beyond that. So in the beginning, I tried to figure out what it was that had created this within me. Let me make it clear: it was not that I set out to do this. It just seemed to be the natural order of things. It was placed in front of me to look at the beginning, which turned out to be my family (read "familiar") of origin.

I had been studying my family most of my life. So I began to understand the powerful dynamics of the dysfunctional family system. I gained knowledge of the different roles that each person in that system played out, at least in how I saw my role within my family. It all seemed so accurate. I did gain great understanding, yet it did not seem to ease my emotional discomfort. Now I can see it didn't change my judgment of myself. In a strange way, it almost validated it.

I can see now my dis-ease was due to powerful self-identification. Obviously, I was not willing to let go of it at that time. In gaining some understanding of the science related to the energy that flows to me and through me, there has been even more acceptance of how all this works. Yet even with all that, it seems that my judgment has shifted only slightly. Fortunately, I have a support system that honors my expansion and that differs from the habit and identity that no longer serves my expansion.

So even though the environment of my past serves as an easy vehicle to focus judgment on, my desire to be neutral, to be in a place of inner peace and calm, has grown. As I practice and work on being present in the moment, I create a different kind of discomfort. The shift from judgment, good or bad, and the trust that all that is around me is in perfect order, creates an expanded shift within me. I believe that the grieving of the loss of the old self, the shifting of old perception and belief that I used to hold on to in order to define myself, is being released. It seems contrary to honor the discomfort that I have judged so harshly in the recent past.

I do want to own this: the discomfort of the moment is so much different than the incredible pain that I carried with me most my life. Incrementally, the low-vibration energy that is being released served my survival but also caused me much pain. I now understand it kept me connected to my past, yet opened me up to an expanded connection of higher energy and vibration.

As I let go of the judgment, the discomfort, and the flow of this transformation, I find the calm and peace I have longed for. Searching for it in substance and relationships outside myself no longer works for me as it did when I was working so hard to just survive. When all was in order to define what was always within me, it remained judgment and perception based from my past that kept me from embracing my center. It is time to accept the feedback I have given others to be of support to them in their healing:

"You are incapable of doing it wrong, stop judging it. Just keep doing what you have been doing to the best of your ability. Continue to radiate from the center that is your true power, the love from your heart."

As I make this statement towards my SELF, I offer it to all who are reading or hearing this.

Blessings to all of us as we walk this path of our own expansion and healing.

# THE QUEST CONTINUES

I have been speaking for well over 20 years on topics related to Emotional Detox, from Twelve Step meetings in the beginning, to treatment and spiritual teaching centers, and speaking with numerous individuals. In recent years I have served as an outside trainer at a health care agency in Phoenix, Arizona. I even went to Seattle, Washington to do a talk at an agency there.

It would seem that I had a lot to teach; the reality is that I have a lot to learn.

When I am doing some of my talks, I often hear myself say things I had not realized I thought or even accepted. I say these things as what I believe. Case in point: I had accepted that I was not very intelligent or smart. This was true way before I realized I am dyslexic. I would concentrate so hard and literally watch the teachers' mouths in school, trying to absorb the information they were offering. I had also rationalized some of this, saying I was still processing the fighting and violence of my parents that would have gone on the night before. The two together (dyslexia and lack of concentration) created a synergistic effect, coupled with the powerful perception that I had created about myself: I was not smart.

So many years passed. My life was in a complete transition. I started doing something that I was incapable of doing in school. I began to research and study. This has come clear to me only as I am writing this. With all the different types of modalities that I sought out, I was always drawn towards the science or physics of dis-ease/recovery, cause and effect, and the energy in motion (or emotion) that flows though us.

So back to my case in point. I was speaking at a treatment center when I heard someone say, "There was excitement with the fact that I would not ever stop the ability to continue to learn, if not on this side or in this life, but will continue to the next." I actually stopped, turned around, looked behind me, then back. I asked out loud, "Who said that?" That statement was contrary to all that I believed and perceived about myself. I was not really able to embrace the power of the shift that was beginning within myself, to own my ability to give my *self* permission to redefine my intelligence.

As more time passed, I also accepted that what I had considered a disorder called dyslexia had been redefined as a special way my mind works. It has allowed me to look at my process of healing in a more positive way. It is okay that I see the world, the universe, and spirit the way I do. It is okay to have new perceptions and beliefs toward the other souls who surround me. I have very rarely felt above others, but I can choose to not feel less than. This is a real gift even though there are still times when, given the energy that I feel from some, I may have some old emotional reaction. I am grateful that this is fairly rare in my life today.

So here's another example of offering a statement to someone, to be considered as a concept to empower one's own healing. I was working with someone who was dealing with some issues within her family. At one point she brought up a personal issue related to a possible health problem. When medical issues come up, if I believe the person might benefit, I refer him or her to a colleague who is a major support of my own healing and transformation. He is a medical intuitive and is gifted in many other modalities, including communicating with animals.

So as I began to explain what he does, I looked to see what her reaction might be, knowing that many still are skeptical and are fearful of out-of-the-box ways of healing. She seemed to be interested. As I related what he did, I said this to her, "I hope you are open-minded."

Her response was enthusiastic. "Oh, yes, I am open-minded; you can ask all my friends how open I am."

Then, to my own surprise, I said, "I am not asking about being open to the healing. Most people are open to that. What I'm asking is if you are willing to be open to letting go of what has caused you to create dis-ease?"

Silence followed, from both of us. She then said that this was something to think about. She agreed to see my friend and colleague, and I understand that the session went well. I continued to think of this statement about letting go of disease, even sharing it with others, I think, to find some reaction to it. It was something I said because I needed to hear it. I became more aware, even after all the tremendous gains I had made on my own journey. It is clear just how much resistance I have had. It is easy now to look back and understand I had been reluctant to let go of dis-ease. So, I have come to have gratitude for the many ways I have become open to letting go of those beliefs and perceptions related to ignorance. I once held those beliefs in order to survive but came to realize they have caused me dis-ease.

So it turned out the question I asked another to consider was a lesson for me—to show me that I am still as much a student as I am the teacher. I am open to this as a part of my new life. Over the years I have been confronted by others with the question, "Are you a healer?" For a long time I resisted answering. I felt they were asking because they wanted me to heal them. Or the question was a set-up to challenge me. I resisted answering "yes" because I did not want to have responsibility for anyone else's healing, although I know now I could not do that anyway. Now I understand that my tendency to take on others' emotions and issues and make them my own also caused my resistance to answering that question: "Are you a healer?"

At some point I started to accept that I am the only one I can influence to expanded healing. Yet as I expand my own healing, I am beginning to understand it will affect others, just as much as when I was radiating dis-ease. So I begin to accept my role as a healer, with this qualification: I am a healer, but I have one primary client, and that is *me*. Even while in the role of teaching, it is more important to me to always be the student. I accept that everyone is capable of being my teacher, if I am open.

## Childlike/Childish

There are so many aspects of this process of change and redefining myself that have been—for whatever reason—distant from my understanding. "Confused" might be another way to define it. I don't always mean things in an intellectual mode. I feel that I have a great understanding but, for me, it is a tactile experience, something I can touch or feel, not just know intellectually. This is how my art comes through me and the same way I develop my business in the pool industry in Phoenix. A very special member of my family of choice, Randy, offered another term to describe what I mean: it is visceral, a connection, literally in my gut.

Experiencing the lessons that are on my path as an emotional experience makes it sometimes discomforting to grasp parts of this process. One of these concepts is the separation of being childish or childlike.

Although my sister described me as a happy child, I do not have any recollection of that. Going back to that word visceral, I have no visceral connection to feeling happy in my childhood. What seemed to fit my connection to that time was when my sister-in-law described to me many years ago her first impression of me as a child. She said that when she first came over to our home, I was outside standing alone. As she gazed at me and picked up the energy I was radiating, she wondered why this little boy was so serious, sad, and angry.

Now this is what I could and did relate to. I was in my mid-thirties and relatively new into my process, at least a couple of years. I had this overwhelming feeling of sadness wash through me as she made her observation of me as a child. I have always believed my sister-in-law to be gifted in the assessments of those she encountered in her life. She was at that time outside the family system, and I could gain insight from a perspective that was not subject to my family system.

My brother, who is fifteen years older than I am, shared something that validated more of how I was perceived. He said that on occasion he would take me with him in the car to meet girls. I guess I was a cute kid and he felt it would help. He shared that some of the girls would also question why I seemed so serious and sad.

So what has this to do with childish or childlike? What has come up for me is my own living perception and very twisted concept of what it is to feel like a child. It has taken writing this to help me put this in perspective for myself and of myself. This has opened me up to be aware of other behaviors that I used to survive.

At some point I believe I realized that rage and tantrums did not work, so I developed a behavior of playing the role of a victim. When I was in grade school a buddy and I got into some kind of problem on the playground. Told to wait in one of the classrooms to find out our punishment, I began to shift to my victim demeanor. My childhood friend looked at me and asked "What are you doing?" His question makes me realize that my entire persona was shifting.

Perhaps if I got little enough I would not get hurt. We were in our forties when my childhood friend shared with me his perception of me in those grade school days. I was shocked at how long I have carried this identity throughout my life. I was equally impressed that this person was so perceptive, even as child.

No wonder I have trouble conceiving the difference between childish or childlike. The habits I created to deal with my environment were far from the fun and happy aspects of childlike. It had always been so far away I could not even dream of it as a concept.

So I had resistance to any of the warm, fuzzy concepts of being childlike. In this process of healing, I've felt real regret and even much harsh judgment toward myself due to the distance I felt from others when they shared their ability to express childlike attributes. Yet at another level I am beginning to accept that this is the way it was. Nothing can change the past: regret, anger, frustration, or the judgment of it only serves to keep me stuck in it.

I am a person who needs a visceral experience in order to have some connection. Not having it confuses me as to what I want. Some of my first teachers asked, "What is the feeling you are having?" I had no idea how to respond. Similarly, up until recently, some would ask, "What do you want?" Again I struggled to even know that. It now makes sense why it has been difficult for me to just imagine. Now I know to go back to what was really my first desire when I started this process: to get to a place where I could just feel good inside my own skin.

As I move into that place, sometimes with lots of resistance to letting go of the old self, I can be more open to experiencing childlike as opposed to the emotionally childish habits that helped me to survive but held me back from the peace I want and deserve in my life today.

So it is mine to create my healing based on my way of understanding, and not judge my process because of the way others choose their process. We will each find our way. I am more accepting of my process, even when at times the discomfort is sometimes still powerful, by not getting caught up on another's process. As hard as I have been on myself, those comparisons have only complicated my frustration, which in turn activated my habitual childish reactions.

I know that I am on a journey toward the center of my *being*, and that I am resonating an energy of *Love of Self.* There was a time not long ago when I could not even imagine having the ability to make that statement.

My quest continues. Come join me.

# ACKNOWLEDGMENTS

I would like to acknowledge the two souls who were vehicles that brought forth a child. That child created powerful ways to negotiate and survive. I honor that little boy who grew into a man with the power and courage to choose to recreate and redefine himself. He attracted and surrounded himself with those who would support him and co-create with him as he moved through the process of Emotional Detox that is at the core of healing. So my greatest acknowledgement is to SELF.

As part of my healing path, I offer my heartfelt gratitude to those who have co-created my expanded healing, who have been attracted into my life and support me on my path of redefining SELF. This includes those who modeled how and, equally, those who modeled "how not."

I see each of your individual souls as a cell within the collective organism that I call my Family of Choice. This organism is focused on healing rather than dis-ease. My hope is that each of you knows my heartfelt energy surrounds you. To those who may not know, I send love, light, and healing energy.

## ABOUT THE AUTHOR

Having challenged himself with the powerful question, "WHO AM I?", David Fraijo searched for the answer to why he perceived himself in the ways that he did. After an incremental process of Emotional Detox, in which he redefined his perceptions of SELF, his expanded healing allowed him to move past a dysfunctional childhood and the addictions that helped him survive.

Negative energy attracted negative situations and relationships. David now radiates a healing energy that invites others to seek their own path toward positive change through Emotional Detox.

A native of Arizona, David's roots go back on his mother's side to working the land in Territorial days and a rich history of mining in Jerome and Superior on his father's side. David continues a family tradition of business ownership with his pool deck company. He also works as an artist, author, life coach, and inspirational speaker. David can be reached at **emotionaldetox@yahoo.com**